Corporate Taxation
in the Netherlands Antilles

Corporate Taxation in the Netherlands Antilles

by

F. DAMIAN LEO
Loyens & Volkmaars
Curaçao

ANTONIO A. AMADOR
Touche Ross International
New York

1978
Springer-Science+Business Media, B.V.

Cover design: Pieter J. van der Sman

ISBN 978-90-200-0540-0 ISBN 978-94-017-4367-9 (eBook)
DOI 10.1007/978-94-017-4367-9

Originally published by Kluwer, Deventer in 1978

Contents

Introduction

Corporate income taxation in the Netherlands Antilles is embodied in a law of a total of 57 articles, i.e. Articles 1 to 54 and Articles 8A, 9A and 14A. The law is divided into nine chapters.

Chapter 1 (Articles 1 to 16) contains the substantive portion of the law and Chapters II to IX are the procedural articles, the penal sanctions, transistory and effectivity provisions.

Articles 8A, 9A, 14 and 14A are the Articles which substantially regulate the taxation of off-shore or non-resident companies.

It should be noted however, that all the other articles of the law together with additional legislation, e.g. Guaranty Law of 1969, (exept when specifically excluded) are likewise applicable to off-shore companies. Thus, rules on allowable and allocable deductions, loss carry forward, assessment and collection are identical for both off-shore and on-shore companies.

It is a tribute to the legislators who drafted and enacted the present law and the officials who execute it that two totally divergent taxation regimes work in acceptable harmony.

History and Background

Prior to the introduction of the law on corporate income taxation in 1940, there existed one law on personal income and on profits of entities, regulated in the Income Tax law of 1906.

Said law was based on the so called source-income-fiction theory. Income or profits from the previous year are considered as basis for tax over the subsequent year. The present law is based on the 'real profit' theory embodied under Article 3, which states that the actual profit has to be taxed. The separation of corporate income taxation came in 1940, with the introduction of the present law, while the Personal Income Tax law was enacted three years later.

The Indonesian Corporate Income Tax Law of 1925 has served as a model for the Antillean Profits Law Tax of 1940. The present law has a non-personal character which means that the entity is placed on the background, and the focus is on the profit of such entity. In principle, the worldwide profit of a resident entity is subject to the profits tax. For non-resident entities, however, the law only applies if these entities have a permanent establishment, or own real estate situated within the Netherlands Antilles.

Both laws, as amended, exist today.

However, the Profit Tax Law of 1940 has been subjected to very substantial revisions, for example, the articles dealing with the holding companies.

On the other hand, there are some articles in the law, which can be qualified as antiquated. The articles regulating the computation of the net taxable income have not kept pace with the dynamic developments in business and industry for the last 50 years.

The translation of the law into English is a compromise between literal and free translation.[1] The authors have tried to catch and impart the meaning of the Dutch text without deviating from the crisp but sweeping generality of the original. The law is written with grand brevity rather than incisive precision. This malleable approach unfamiliar to other jurisdictions particularly the US is typical of Dutch legal language which often leaves to judicial interpretation, rather than the use of comprehensive enumeration, the full force and impact of the law. The reason is rooted in the legal system.

Mr. P. Den Boer, deputy judge of the Court of Tax Appeals in The Hague, in an article[2] explained that 'the meaning and spirit of the law often prevail over a strictly grammatical interpretation'. It may happen that the judge through interpretation attributes a sense and meaning to legal provisions which the legislator may never have thought of or are even fully contrary to what he may have meant. Historical, systematic, teological and even analogical interpretations are much used to arrive at an equitable and reasonable decision, which, rather than legal certainty, is the aim.

'This approach to law in general also applies to tax laws, especially those which have a strong bearing on the economic aspects of the social phenomena. Although care has to be taken that the levying of the tax is strictly based on law (Art. 188 of the Dutch Constitution) the law itself is seen as a basis for flexible interpretation. A consequence of this is that Dutch tax laws sometimes may be very abstract and short, making use of general terms or referring to general notions'.

It is with the foregoing in mind that the authors translated the law. They have extensively consulted other, perhaps better translations.

1. For reasons of convenience titles are given to the articles by the editors in this translation. They are missing in the original text.
2. Anti Avoidance Measures in The Netherlands, Tax Havens and Measures Against Tax Evasion and Avoidance in the EEC, edited by J.F. Avery Jones, Associated Business Programmes Ltd. 1974.

INTRODUCTION

This book is an attempt not only to bridge a language barrier but it essays to emphasize that in this country of six small islands in the Caribbean many refer to simply as a 'Tax Haven' there is a system of taxation tested by time and molded by practice and practitioners, responsive to a degree, to the exigencies of changing economic realities but tempered by what is fair and will endure.

Curaçao, December 1977

Chapter I: Subject, Amount and Tax Liability

Article 1: Subject

1. A tax under the name 'Winstbelasting' (Profit Taxation) shall be levied on:

a. The profits of corporations, limited partnerships, joint stock companies, companies or associations, the capitalization of which is divided, totally or partially into shares, co-operative societies and mutual insurance societies, having their statutory seat within the Netherlands Antilles.

b. The profits of associations having their statutory seat within the Netherlands Antilles, the capitalization of which is not divided into shares, and of foundations engaged in trade or business other than those which exclusively serve the general public interest.

c. The profits of entities having this statutory seat without the Netherlands Antilles (including corporations, partnerships or associations, the capitalization of which is divided, totally or partially into shares) gained from trade or business conducted through a permanent establishment within the Netherlands Antilles, or from immovable properties situated within the Netherlands Antilles, as well as gains from receivables not in the ordinary course of business of the company, in so far as the principal is secured by mortgage upon said immovables.

2. Whether a corporation, partnership, joint stock company, foundation, association or entity is established within the Netherlands Antilles shall be determined according to the circumstances of the given case. However, should the incorporation or formation be made pursuant to the laws of the Netherlands Antilles, the statutory seat shall always be construed as being within the Netherlands Antilles.

3. A trade or business shall also be construed to mean the performance of all activities, operations or services of whatever nature.

Any form of entity either with shareholders, members or holders of an undivided interest, or an entity either with a separate juridical personality or not, is taxable under the broad scope of this Article. The Supreme Court held that 'also associations without a juridical personality in so far as they are engaged in business are taxable'.[1]

The mere creation of a foundation does not exempt said foundation from tax. To be exempt, a foundation should serve the general public interest ('algemeen maatschappelijk belang'). The explanatory memorandum of the law states that 'It is not the purpose of the association or foundation but it is the character of the enterprise that is decisive'.[2] Thus, a business enterprise serving the general public interest, like a public utility, even though structured as a foundation is taxable. The conduct of the enterprise must be imbued with an ideal or altruistic purpose for a foundation to be exempt from taxation.

Foundations although possessed with a separate legal personality are not registered[3] in any governmental agency in the Netherlands Antilles. A foundation is created by Notarial Deed and, provided it serves the general public interest as abovementioned, no tax ruling from the Inspectorate of Taxes is required for it to be exempt from tax. However, it may be prudent to secure a Ruling if the donation to the foundation is to be exempt from donor's tax or the foundation, exempt from donee's tax.

Foundations which are exempt need not lodge annual tax returns with the Inspector of Taxes.

Profits of entities situated without the Netherlands Antilles are taxable if a trade or business is conducted through a permanent establishment within the Netherlands Antilles. The concept of a permanent establishment is not defined in the statute. There is a permanent establishment if a trade or business is conducted through a place of management, office, branch, factory or workshop, mine or building site. It does not include the mere storage, display or delivery of goods or merchandise. Neither does it include a fixed place of business maintained solely for the purpose of the purchase of goods or for collecting information.

It is significant to note that unlike other jurisdictions, in the Netherlands Antilles, the length of time of the conduct of the trade or business is not a factor to consider in the determination of the existence of a permanent establishment.

A person who acts on behalf of an entity situated without the Netherlands Antilles if he has and habitually exercises the authority to con-

1. Supreme Court decision of 15 January 1938 (Arresten Hoge Raad van 15 januari 1938, B. Nos. 4680-6756).
2. Explanatory Notes ('Memorie van Toelichting') on the Bill of the proposed Profit Tax Law of 1940, Staten van Curacao 1939-1940-39, No. 3, p. 1 (hereinafter cited as MvT 1939-1940-39).
3. The law requiring registration of Foundations has been adopted by Parliament (Staten van de Nederlands Antillen) but has yet to be promulgated.

clude contracts on behalf of the entity shall constitute a permanent establishment, except if the contracts are simply for the purpose of purchase of goods or merchandise.[4]

'Immovable Property' for the purpose of this article may be defined as '... buildings, land, trees and ungathered fruits and anything which is permanently attached or nailed to a building. Further it includes, by virtue of its purpose, machineries in factories or workshops, fertilizers destined to enrich the land, pigeons homing to a particular area and fishes in ponds'. Finally, the term 'Immovable Property' includes also the following 'rights to Immovable Property: the usufruct and use of real property, easements, building and planting rights, tenancy rights and perpetual leasehold rights at a fixed price, and ground rent.'[5]

The taxation of companies established in the Netherlands Antilles but also doing business without the Netherlands Antilles will be discussed under the commentary on Article 12.

In the determination of whether an entity has a permanent establishment, the facts rather than the law shall determine the 'circumstances of the given case' as referred to under paragraph 2 of this Article.

For purposes of taxation, the factual considerations to take into account are different from the considerations in determining the civil law concept of domicile. A business enterprise has two important aspects for the purposes of this Article. The situs of where policy decisions are made and the situs of its operations. In general, the former (where effective management is conducted) is a decisive factor.

The place of operations also weighs heavily, as well as the place where the meetings of shareholders are convened. Such factors as registration with a Trade Register, listing in a telephone directory and the address used in the usual correspondence by the entity are circumstances closely examined.

The foregoing premises notwithstanding, if an entity is constituted pursuant to the laws of the Netherlands Antilles, said entity shall be considered as having its statutory seat within the Netherlands Antilles.[6]

4. For a comprehensive definition of 'permanent establishment', see Art. 5 of the United Kingdom – Kingdom of the Netherlands Tax Convention.
5. Decree on Corporate Income Taxation 1942, Art. 21, No. 9 (Besluit Vennootschapbelasting 1942, Art. 21, No. 9).
6. J.J. de Klerck and D.J. Muller, Besluit op de Vennootschapsbelasting, wet op de Herkapitalisatie, Wet Richtige Heffing, Uittreksel Gemeentewet eighth edition, A.E. Kluwer, Deventer, p. 98ij (hereinafter cited as De Klerck and Muller).

Article 2: Exemptions

The following shall be exempt from taxation:

a. The profits of the entities referred to in Article 1, paragraph 2 under letter c derived from the transportation of persons and goods by sea and air between ports within the Netherlands Antilles and ports without the Netherlands Antilles.

b. The profits of the entities referred to in paragraph 1, Article 1 derived from the purchase, sale, storage and delivery of oil and oil products if and insofar as the purchase, sale, storage and delivery are effected by or through the entities referred to in Article 9.

c. The profits of pension funds, savings funds, provident funds, burial funds, sickness funds and benevolent funds which have been created for the benefit of employees, former employees and/or their dependants, provided that these funds are established within the Netherlands Antilles and have a juridical personality. The question whether a Fund complies with the requirements for exemption shall insofar as necessary be determined in accordance with the circumstances of each case.

Foreign entities carrying goods and persons from without the Netherlands Antilles into a port within the Netherlands Antilles or vice-versa are exempt from taxation. The rationale of the exemption is based on the principle that the carrier itself is an extension of the territory of the country of the carrier.

Letter B of this article has lost its efficacy through the amendment of Article 9 of this law.[7]

Funds created for the benefit of employees, former employees and/or their dependents, (dependents have been interpreted to mean minor children or the widow or widower of an employee or former employee) shall qualify for exemption provided said Funds are constituted according to the laws of the Netherlands Antilles and pursuant to said laws have a juridical personality.

In practice, it is prudent to secure a Tax Ruling from the Inspector of Taxes to qualify a Fund as exempt from taxation. Said Ruling will not usually be issued if the shareholders, members or participants of the Fund can withdraw their contribution at anytime. There should be a fixed time of maturity eitherbased on the age of the participant or a specific time or the happening of a condition subsequent such as the incapacity of the shareholder, member or participant. In general, the contribution to the Fund may not be used by the contributor to secure a loan.

7. Official Gazette, 1975, No. 29 (P.B. 1975, No. 29).

Profits made by a Fund from mortgages are exempt from taxation. Contributions made to a tax-exempt Fund is a deductible expense from the personal taxable income of the contributor.

Article 3: Fiscal Year

The tax shall be levied upon each fiscal year or, in the absence thereof, upon each calendar year.

A fiscal year consists of 12 months or 365 days. A company at the time of incorporation may have a fiscal year of over 12 months but not over 18 months or a shorter fiscal year of over 6 months but less than 12 months. Thus, for a company incorporated in the month of July, with a fiscal year corresponding to the calendar, the incorporators may choose to end its first fiscal year on the 31st of December following the year of incorporation.

Inversely, a company incorporated in the month of May will have its first fiscal year-end on the 31st of December of the same year or any month of the following calendar year thereafter up to the 30th of April.

A company's fiscal year is fixed in its Deed of Incorporation and not by its management.

If a company has its fiscal year ending on the 31st of October and the same company is liquidated on the 20th of November following the end of its fiscal year, a consolidated statement cannot be made to include the extra 20 days. Two sets of financial statements will have to be made, the first to cover the regular fiscal year and the second from the end of the fiscal year to the date of liquidation.

Foundations whose constitution does not provide for a fiscal year are assessed on each calendar year, i.e. if the foundation is taxable.

Article 4: Definition of the Term 'Profits'

1. The term 'profits' shall be construed to mean the net aggregate sum of benefits under whatever name and in whatever form realized out of a trade or business or realized from capital employed outside the ordinary course of trade or business.
2. The benefits (referred to in the preceding paragraph) shall be construed to include the benefits derived from the alienation of property that is not intended for sale and in general, all the benefits derived from such property even if the benefits are realized after the trade or business have ceased their operations.

3. The benefits (referred to in the preceding paragraphs) shall likewise include the undistributed profits of corporations referred to in Article 8A, Article 14 or Article 14A, provided the profits directly or indirectly accrue to an entity refered to under letter a of paragraph 1 of Article 1, unless the entity itself is a corporation referred to in Article 8A, Article 14 or Article 14A.
4. In the event of liquidation, the increment in value of property distributed to those entitled thereto shall be considered a benefit within the meaning of this Article.
5. The increment of value as referred to in paragraph 4 shall be the difference between the selling price of the property distributed and its fiscal book value at the time of transfer, it being understood that if the selling price is lower than the fair market value or cash price the latter shall be substituted for the selling price.

The law uses the words 'under whatever name and in whatever form' to emphasize the term profit which within the meaning of this ordinance is a material concept, independent from the subjective view of interested parties; neither is it dependent upon the manner the books of account are kept.[8] The norms of normal and acceptable commercial practice should be applied in the determination of profits.[9] By the term profit the law also includes benefits derived from capital invested not in the ordinary course of business. Thus, if an entity engaged purely in the production of goods and invests its funds in bonds, the benefits derived from this investment, even if under corporate law, the investment is ultra vires, shall under this present law be added to the taxable income of the company.

In the computation of an entity's taxable profits, the 'guilder is a guilder' theory is applicable and no allocable deduction for inflation is ever allowed.

The books of account of corporations must always be kept on an 'accrual basis' and not on a 'cash basis'. A reserve for a doubtful source of revenue is allowed following norms of normal and acceptable commercial practice. Bad debts are allowable deductions when incurred. Thus, a receivable which remains uncollected after the lapse of, e.g. one year, depending on the nature of the transaction may be written-off as a bad debt the following year.

Under paragraph 2 of this article, an example of 'property not intended for sale' is a car provided by a company to an employee and

8. Mr. Dr. B.J.F. Steinmetz, De Indische Vennootschapsbelasting (Ordonnantie op de vennootschapsbelasting 1925), H.D. Tjeenk Willink & Zoon N.V., Haarlem, 1933, P. 252 (hereinafter cited as Steinmetz).
9. See comments Steinmetz, p. 269.

sold to the employee at a price higher than its book value. The difference between the selling price and the book value is a taxable benefit for the company. As another example, the proceeds of a fire insurance policy (in so far as they exceed the book value of the property lost by fire) is a taxable benefit in the hands of the company despite the fact that the company has ceased its operations due to the fire, or for whatever reason.[10]

Paragraph 3 of this article refers to Articles 8A, 14 and 14A, the articles under this law which grant certain taxation advantages to companies fulfilling certain requirements of the law and governmental regulations. Detailed discussion will be made in the commentary under these articles. Paragraph 3 of this article, however, makes it clear that the law will follow the principle of fiscal transparency and disregard the existance of a separate legal entity. Profits of corporations operating under the fiscal advantages of Articles 8A, 14 and 14A when accruing directly or indirectly to any entity as defined under the very first article of this law, shall be fully taxable. The exception is when the receipient of the benefit is a corporation operating under the very same Articles 8A, 14 and 14A.

Paragraph 4 makes an exception to the general rule that only realized gains are taxable. In case of liquidation, if assets are distributed in kind to those entitled thereto, the increase in value of those assets distributed in kind shall be considered as a taxable benefit albeit an unrealized benefit at the time of distribution.

If the liquidator before the distribution should sell the distributable assets for cash, then obviously, the benefit is realized and therefore taxable.

The difference between the selling price and the book value of a given asset is considered as its 'increment in value'. If the selling price is lower than the book value, the selling price shall be disregarded and the fair market value considered as the selling price.

If the selling price is higher than the book value but lower than the fair market value, the latter shall again be considered as the selling price.

Article 5: Allowable Deductions

1. In the computation of the net aggregate sum of benefits referred to under Article 4, the gross benefits shall be reduced by the costs incurred for the acquisition, collection, and maintenance of said benefits, including such costs for constituting the entity and any increase of its capital as referred to in paragraph 2 of this article.

10. See comments Steinmetz, pp. 34-35.

2. The costs incurred in the constitution of the entity and the increase of its capital shall be an allowable deduction which may be taken at any time in the manner the books of account are kept, it being understood that the sum deducted over a number of years shall in no case exceed the total costs incurred.
3. The gross benefits of the entity shall furthermore be reduced by depreciation as an allowable deduction for the decrease of the utility-value of an asset used in the ordinary course of business, as well as a deduction for irrecoverable receivables related to the ordinary course of business, following normal and acceptable commercial practice.
4. The gross benefits of capital employed not in the ordinary course of business shall be reduced by depreciation as an allowable deduction for the expiration of rights limited by a term.

Article 4 of this law defines what is a taxable benefit to an entity while the present article enumerates the allowable deductions. In an ordinary entity engaged in the production of goods, such items as cost of goods sold, selling and administrative expenses including research and development costs are allowable deductions to taxable income. In an ordinary investment company, costs for investment management, administration and custodianship, as well as registrar and transfer agency fees, including directors' salaries, legal and auditing expenses are allowable deductions.

Paragraph 2 provides for the maximum deduction when incorporation fees are amortized over a number of years, and it also grants the entity the choice of the amount per year and the number of years of amortization.

Depreciation

Durable capital goods as opposed to consumable goods are depreciable under the law. Allowance for depreciation is deductible from the cost price of the depreciable item and not on its fair market value. The guilder is a guilder theory is again made applicable.

In the Netherlands Antilles no depreciation tables are used. Normal and acceptable commercial practice is the measure utilized.

Thus, the generally acceptable practice in depreciating a new concrete office building is a maximum of 2.5% per year straight line. Plumbing and electrical installation are not usually depreciated separately, although air-conditioning may be entered as a separate depreciable item. Leasehold improvements are depreciable according to the term of the lease contract or over their useful lives, whichever is less.

Movables like automobiles are depreciated according to its use. Car rental agencies may depreciate its fleet in three years, office service cars in four years and a Managing Directors' car in five.

Depletion allowance is allowed following normal and acceptable commercial practice bearing in mind that the allowance is based on the cost price of the depletable asset.

In the determination of the 'utility value of an asset' a distinction should be made between an asset's economic value and its utility or technical value. Thus, an extensive library of an international tax consultant in the Netherlands Antilles, in the case of a total change on the very basis of taxation in the islands may have a residual value for book collectors but its utility value to the tax consultant is nil and may thus be totally written off.

It should be noted, however, that an asset can only be depreciated on its cost or historical value but never on its replacement value.

Finally, in commercial leasing, a distinction must be made between the legal and the beneficial owner of the depreciable asset. In general it is the beneficial owner who shall be allowed the deduction for depreciation. A sound criteria to use is to answer the question to whom does the title to the asset pass at the termination of the lease?

The party who acquires the property is usually allowed the depreciation deduction.

Article 6: Non-deductible Expenses

1. Expenditure for the purchase, erection, improvement or alteration of land, building, machinery, equipment and other properties utilized in the trade or business, expenditure for the take over, expansion, improvement or alternation of the trade or business and other expenditure of a similar nature, shall not be allowable deductions, unless the said expenditure is incurred in the ordinary course of business.

2. No deduction shall be allowed:

a. For the creation or increase of any reserve fund.

b. For interest on the equity capital of the entity.

c. For the interest on monies raised or borrowed and for expenditure made for the use of properties made available in whatever form, if, either because of the fact that the interest and expenditure redound to the benefit, directly or indirectly, to one or more persons or entities, solely or jointly with others who are entitled, directly or indirectly, to more than half of the issued capital, or because of the circumstances it must be assumed that the juridical basis of the interest and payment are not in accordance with the generally accepted norms of commercial practice in providing monies and other properties had there been no special relationship between the parties.

d. For taxes on profit levied within the Netherlands Antilles, and for taxes levied in whatever form without the Netherlands Antilles on profits derived from within the Netherlands Antilles.

e. For distributions of profits, including distributions out of or any surplus of the business or of any subdivision of the business in whatever name and in whatever form, regardless of whether the distributions are due and payable or not, with the exception, however, of distributions made to the Netherlands Antilles other than in the latter's capacity of shareholder, and of distributions made to others in consideration of services rendered except for members of the supervisory board, delegates, managing directors, general managers or managing partners.

This article enumerates the expenses incurred by an entity which are not allowable deductions to its gross income.

Paragraph 1 distinguishes capital expense and ordinary expense. Paragraph 2 refers to expenses which are considered by the law as having been incurred but should be disallowed because it constitutes a benefit to the shareholder or participant of the entity.

Taxes levied on the profits of the entity are likewise covered under Paragraph 2.

Expense for durable capital items is not deductible as such but the capital items may be depreciated as discussed in the previous article. There are, however, capital items which are durable and may be used over several years, e.g. rulers, wrenches, etc. but because of the small amount of the expence are considered an ordinary business expense deductible as such, the rule of 'minima non curat praetor' is applied on such small expenses.

Paragraph 2, letter a, disallows a charge to income for the creation of a reserve fund. The words 'reserve fund' do not accurately describe the intent of the law. The name of the charge to income is not decisive but it is the nature of the charge which is important. The portion of the income which normally would have constituted a part of the profits if set aside to cover a future undetermined expense for loss or investment is what is contemplated by the law as a non deductible reserve. An investment allowance as well as reserves are allowable deductions (see Article 9) in specific cases, e.g. shipping companies, but this will be discussed under the article on shipping.

In some jurisdications, a normal yield on invested capital is allowed as a charge to taxable income. The principle, however, followed in the

Netherlands Antilles is that all the net material benefits accruing to the entity are taxable. Thus, the percentage of the profits paid to preferred shareholders is not an allowable deduction. The payment made by an entity to holders of its profit certificates ('Winstbewijs') is not an allowable deduction.

Only real interest expense paid to banks or interest paid 'at arms length' to bonafide creditors or debenture holders of an entity is allowed as a charge to taxable income.

An entity's interest expense or other expenditures are not allowable deductions if said disbursements redound to the benefit of persons or entities who control more than 50% of the issued and outstanding capital of the paying entity notwithstanding the fact that said benefits redound:

1. Directly or indirectly, *or*
2. Solely or jointly with others as long as there is more than 50% control of the paying entity by the payee.

The benefit may be assumed to have redounded to the benefit of the payee of the interest or expenditure if:

1. The interest expense or other expenditure was disbursed not in accordance with the generally accepted norms of commercial practice, *or*
2. There is a special relationship between the payor and the payee of the interest expense or other expenditure.

The law is clear and explicit in its prohibition against any payment of interest or any expense to any person or entity that controls more than 50% of the entity wherefrom interest or payment is received.

Indirect control of the paying entity may be illustrated by the following examples:

a. 1. Company A controls 100% company B.
   2. Company B controls 100% Company C.

Interest due to Company A for a loan it extends to Company C is not an allowable deduction for Company C.

b. 1. Company A controls 100% companies B and C.
   2. Companies B and C each have a 30% interest in Company D.

Interest due to Company A for a loan it extends to Company D is not an allowable deduction for Company D.

c. 1. Company A has 40% interest in Company B and 80% interest in Company C.
   2. Company C has a 25% interest in Company B.

Interest due to Company A for a loan it extends to Company B is not an allowable deduction for Company B as Company A indirectly controls 20% of Company B through its 80% interest in Company C and the 25% interest of Company C in Company B. The 20% added to its direct 40% interest constitutes more than 50% control of Company B.

d. 1. Companies A and B each have a 50% interest in Company C.
   2. Company C controls 100% company D.

Interest due to Company A for a loan it extends Company D *is* a deductible expense for Company D because Company A indirectly controls only 50% and *not more than* 50% of Company D.

In the foregoing examples, the interest due may be substituted by any expenditure made for the use of property and the same rule will apply. Thus, instead of a loan, Company A in the foregoing examples makes available machines or equipment. The rule of *more than* 50% control will be applied because the law will assume that the interest or expenditure are in fact hidden dividends because of the nature of the transaction *and* the presence of a special relationship between the parties. One must note that when there is 50% control or less, then two elements must be present, i.e. the non-conformity of the transaction to generally accepted commercial practice and the presence between the parties of a special relationship.

In example D above, if the loan made available to Company D by Company A is at the rate of 15% per annum while the going rate is at 10% for an identical loan transaction, even if the shareholding of Company A is *not* more than 50%, the interest due to Company A from Company D will be disallowed as an interest expense to Company D.

In this example it could well be that only 10% will be an allowable expense for Company D and the 5% disallowed will be *deemed a dividend* in so far as Company A is concerned. Family relationship, either by affinity or consanguinity is considered a special relationship if the nature of the transaction does not appear to be in accordance with the generally accepted norms of commercial practice. A special relationship is both an economic as well as a social vinculum which binds the parties rather than a purely legal bond, i.e. a relationship which is assumed to exist because of the presence of a factor or factors in the transaction which would not have been present had the transaction been entered into by two totally independent persons or entities.

Under letter d of Paragraph 2 of this article what is disallowed are taxes paid on profits either levied in the Netherlands Antilles or without the Netherlands Antilles on profits derived from within the Netherlands Antilles.

The key word under this provision of the law is 'profit'. All other kinds of taxes levied such as real estate assessments, customs duties as well as gift taxes are allowable deductions. The last paragraph of this article has been the source of confusion not only because of the style in which the paragraph is phrased, but also because of the way entities classify distributions other than salary to personnel.

Following the phrasiology of the original Dutch Text Paragraph 2 will read as follows:

'2. No deduction shall be allowed:

a. ...

b. ...

c. ...

d. ...

e. for any distributions of profits ...., with the exception, however, of distributions made to the Netherlands Antilles other than in the latter's capacity of shareholder, and of distributions made to others in consideration of service rendered except for members of the Supervisory Board, delegates, managing directors' etc.

At first glance distributions made to Supervisory Board members are deductible because distributions 'made to others' appear to be a second exception, the first exception being the Netherlands Antilles as a shareholder. Actually 'distribution made to others' is another exception to the rule of non-deductibility of any distributions (the other exception being the Netherlands Antilles as a receipient of the distribution) and distributions to supervisory board members is the exception to the exception.

'Distribution made to others' simply means distribution to employees and/or any other person or entity for services rendered to the entity making the distribution. The law does not distinguish whether the distribution is pursuant to a 'profit sharing' scheme or simply for outstanding services rendered provided the distribution is not to members of the supervisory board, managing directors, etc. etc. in which case the distribution must be an after-tax distribution.

Article 7: Charitable Contributions

1. Gifts made to religious, charitable, cultural, scientific institutions and organizations devoted for the public benefit established in the Netherlands Antilles are allowable deductions to entities referred to under Article 1 Paragraph 1. Documentary evidence of the gift must be submitted.

2. Gifts referred to in the preceding paragraph are deductible up to an aggregate total not exceeding one percent of the profits except for distributions of profits pursuant to Article 11, after

said profits have been reduced by losses carried over as referred to under Article 10, provided they exceed NAf 100.–. The maximum allowable deduction is three per cent of the adjusted profits as herein provided.
3. For the purpose of this Article, gifts shall be an allowable deduction if made out of generosity and not out of necessity and the contributions and benefits do not confer upon the donor any right or claim with a monetary value.

The maximum amounts under Paragraph 2 and the limitations imposed by Paragraph 3 of this article have negated the use of this article in corporate tax planning in the Netherlands Antilles.

Generally, entities make donations to religious and charitable institutions with an undisguised intention of profiting from the donation. By so doing the donation may be allowed as an ordinary business expense for public relations rather than as a donation out of generosity with the concomitant limitations imposed under this present article.

Furthermore under the first paragraph of this article the burden of evidence is shifted from the Government to the donor to show that a donation was in fact made so that the donation will be considered as an allowable deduction.

Article 8: Insurance Companies

1. The profit of any entity referred to in the first paragraph of Article 1 Paragraphs a or b carrying on insurance business, is, if so requested in its tax return and renewable every five years, assessed for any life insurance business at 10 per cent and otherwise (non-life) at 20 per cent of whatever is in any year received as premiums, both periodic or single payment it being understood that premiums related to risks covered without the Netherlands Antilles, received by an entity through means other than a permanent establishment abroad as referred to in Article 12, are, for any life insurance business to be assessed at 5 per cent and all other cases (non-life) at 10 per cent.
2. The profit of any entity referred to in the first paragraph of Article 1 under letter c, which by way of a permanent establishment carries on an insurance business both within and without the Netherlands Antilles is, when the business is transacted in this country where life insurance is concerned, assessed at 10% and otherwise at 20% of:
a. the premiums and capital (single premium) amounts received from insured parties residing or established in the Netherlands

Antilles or received for risks covered within the Netherlands Antilles, and increased by

b. any other amount not yet included in this article, Paragraph 2, under letter a hereinabove, received by the permanent establishment in the Netherlands Antilles on account of insurances effected by it.

3. Any entity referred to in the second paragraph is held to carry on the insurance business within the Netherlands Antilles by means of a permanent establishment, if it effects or has others issue insurance policies and collects or has others collect the incidental premiums due in this country.

4. In the contingencies referred to in the first and the second paragraphs, no deduction shall be allowed for brokerage and other commissions, discounts, reinsurance or other expenses.

5. In deviation of the second paragraph the profits will, if so requested when filing the tax return, and renewable every five years, be assessed at an amount which bears to the whole of the profits of the insurance business the same proportion as the periodic premiums and single payment premiums contemplated by the second paragraph, received in the course of the taxable year, bear to the whole amount received during that year from all insured parties, always provided, however, that all requisite data for making the assessment are submitted together with the tax return and that, if so requested, the said data can be proved to be correct by the production of documentary evidence.

6. For the application of the preceding paragraph the aggregate profits shall be determined in accordance with Articles 4 to 7, inclusive.

7. The 5-year period referred to in Paragraphs 1 and 5 applies to the year when the return is lodged and the years following thereafter.

This article gives insurance companies the option to elect taxation on their gross income or on their net income. Every election once made must be adhered to for a period of five years commencing from the time the corporate income tax return is lodged for the first taxation year of election. In the case of an election to be taxed on the gross income basis, deductions for brokerage and other commissions, discounts and other expenses are obviously not deductible.

In case an election is made for taxation on a gross income basis the rate is 10% of the gross premium received, including receipts from single payment policies on all life policies, and 20% on the total gross premium on all non-life policies.

For insurance entities established without the Netherlands Antilles but doing business within the Netherlands Antilles, the same rates as above apply.

For gross premium income derived from without the Netherlands Antilles, the rate is 5% on life policies and 10% for non-life.

Paragraph 3 of this article defines what is a permanent establishment for insurance entities in the Netherlands Antilles. The issuance of insurance policies and the collection of premiums either as principal or through an agent are construed as a permanent establishment within the Netherlands Antilles.

Paragraph 5 of the present article gives insurance entities established without the Netherlands Antilles but doing business through a permanent establishment within the Netherlands Antilles a third option on the computation of their taxable income. This third option can best be described by the following illustration:

Life Insurance Company 'Riskless' operates worldwide. Riskless has a consolidated worldwide gross premium income from life policies of \$180,000,000. Its branch in the Netherlands Antilles has a gross life premium income of \$2,000,000. Assume that its worldwide consolidated net income is \$5,000,000.

Under Paragraph 5 Riskless in the Netherlands Antilles may opt to be taxed under the following formula:

$$\frac{\text{Netherlands Antilles Gross Premium Income}}{\text{Worldwide Gross Premium Income}} \times \text{Worldwide Net Income}$$

Thus in the foregoing example:

$$\frac{\$\ 2{,}000{,}000}{\$180{,}000{,}000} \times \$5{,}000{,}000 = \$55{,}500 \text{ Taxable Income.}$$

Including the island surcharge the taxation rate on \$55,500 is about 38% resulting in a tax due of about \$18,500.

Had Riskless opted for taxation on a gross income basis of 10% of gross premium income, it would have had a taxable income of \$200,000, or a tax due of about US \$67,000.

In the computation of the gross and/or net income of insurance entities the rules as provided for under the present law, i.e. Articles 4 to 7 are to be applicable. This is a laudible but impractical mandate of the law because it would be difficult if not impossible for a local tax examiner to audit the books of a worldwide insurance company with branches and sets of books located around the world.

Article 8A

This article will be discussed subsequent to Article 14A as its content logically follows Articles 14 and 14A.

Article 9: Oil Refineries

1. Profits of any entity engaged in a petroleum processing enterprise within the Netherlands Antilles shall be assessed according to the conditions laid out in this law, on the understanding that if the profits, after application of Article 15, result in a tax amount due which for an Aruban petroleum processing enterprise does not exceed NAf 37 million and for a Curacao petroleum processing enterprise does not exceed NAf 34.8 million, an additional amount of profit tax shall be assessed for the difference between this tax amount and the amounts of NAf 37 and NAf 34.8 million respectively. As at fiscal year 1975/76 the amounts of 37 + 34.8 million shall be replaced by 28.7 million and 24.4 million respectively.
2. The amount of tax assessed pursuant to Paragraph 1 hereof over and above the amount after the application of Article 15, shall be compensated in the event and inasmuch as the tax levied on the enterprise should exceed in one or more subsequent fiscal years, the amount of NAf 28.7 million and NAf 24.4 million respectively.
3. If in any fiscal year the amounts in so far as the petroleum processing enterprise is concerned decrease, that which was determined in the second paragraph, will cease to be applicable to that enterprise as at the beginning of that fiscal year.

Prior to the amendment of the present law, petroleum processing enterprises in the Netherlands Antilles were taxed in accordance with its productive capacity measured in cubic meters of capacity or production. The present law taxes the industry not unlike any other enterprise based on its profits and applies the normal taxation rates. The unique feature, however, of this article is that a minimum tax amount due is provided for. The law requires a minimum because for budgetary reasons, the Government is of the opinion that it is not sufficient to tax these companies under all circumstances in accordance with their actual profits.[11] Considering the amount of taxes contributed by this indus-

11. Explanatory notes (Memorie van Toelichting) on the Bill to amend the Profit Tax Law of 1940 (P.B. 1965, No. 58), Staten van de Nederlandse Antillen 1974-75, No. 3, page 1.

try, the Government considered and concluded that it cannot properly execute its budgetary plans if its revenues will be based on the uncertain action of the market in oil processing, thus, a minimum tax is provided in the laws.

There are presently two oil refineries in the Netherlands Antilles, Exxon in Aruba and Royal Dutch Shell in Caraçao.

Exxon in Aruba has a minimum tax due of:
NAf 28,700,000 + 15% surtax = NAf 33,005,000.

Shell in Curaçao has a minimum tax due of:
NAf 24,400,000 + 15% surtax = NAf 28,060,000.

The reason for the difference on the minimum is that 'Shell has many more employees in service than the Lago'.[12]

The second paragraph of the present article provides for a system of credit to amounts paid to fill-in the shortfall in the minimum tax due. To illustrate:

Fiscal year	*Taxable income*	*Tax due*	*Minimum tax*	*Credit*
1976	NAF 50,000,000	19,550,000	28,060,000	8,510,000
1977	NAF 90,000,000	35,190,000		
	less credit	(8,510,000)	28,060,000	1,380,000
		26,680,000		
1978	NAF 90,000,000	35,190,000	28,060,000	Nil
	less credit	(1,380,000)		
		33,810,000		

Article 9A: Shipping Companies

1. Entities as referred to under letter a of Paragraph 1 of Article 1, the purpose of which is to carry on the business of ocean-going shipping or aviation business, including the chartering of vessels or aircraft, shall be considered to have derived 80 percent of their profits from without the Netherlands Antilles and determined in accordance with the provisions of this law, except for profits derived from carriage or transportation between ports situated within the Netherlands Antilles, on the conditions as set forth in the third, fourth and fifth paragraphs of this article.
2. The profits derived from without the Netherlands Antilles, as referred to in the preceding paragraph, shall be taxed at the rate of one/tenth of the rates referred to in Article 15.

12. See note 11.

3. The first and second paragraphs of this present Article shall only apply to entities:

a. formed and established under the laws of the Netherlands Antilles, and

b. whose statutory seat is within the Netherlands Antilles, and provided,

c. if and insofar as the entity is engaged in carriage and transportation itself, the day-to-day management is conducted within the Netherlands Antilles.

4. Provided further, the first and second paragraphs of this present article shall only apply if and so long as the ocean-going vessels and aircraft belonging to the business or trade of the entity concerned are registered within the Kingdom of The Netherlands.

5. For the application of the provisions of this Article to any ocean-going vessel or aircraft not registered in the Kingdom of The Netherlands belonging to such entity, a Territorial Order of the Council may, at the request of the said entity, provide and direct that such ocean-going vessel or aircraft be considered as registered within the Kingdom of The Netherlands. Such Order can so provide and direct only if and when the statutory requirements regarding the safety and the care and welfare of the crews obtaining in the country of registration may be deemed to be at least the equivalent to those enforced within the Netherlands Antilles.

6. In this Article by 'ocean-going vessels' is meant: vessels as defined in Section 2 of the Curaçao Decree concerning Certificates of Registration of Ocean-vessels, 1933 ('Curaçaose Luchtvaartbesluit 1935').

7. The provisions of the following paragraphs shall, moreover, exclusively apply to any entity to which Paragraphs 1 and 2 of this article apply on the understanding, however, that if paragraphs 8, 9, 11, and 12 applied, the entity shall keep a regular set of books of account with the requisite annual closings of accounts.

8. a. Notwithstanding the provisions of the third paragraph of Article 5, one/third of the cost of acquisition of ocean-going vessels and aircraft, acquired after 31st December 1960 and prior to 1st January 1981, may be acceleratedly written off at will.

b. The accelerated writing-off referred to hereinabove under Paragraph a, may also be applied to ocean-going vessels and aircraft ordered prior to 1st January 1982.

c. 'Acquisition' includes any improvement of ocean-going vessels and aircraft already previously acquired.

9. a. If in any given year (but not later than 31st December 1980) investments are made in ocean-going vessels or aircraft, eight per cent of the amount invested shall be deducted from the profits of that year as well as of the next following year. By 'investment' is

meant the compliance with obligations entered into for the acquisition or improvement of an ocean-going vessel or aircraft, insofar as such obligations are binding on the taxable entity.
b. The investment allowance referred to hereinbefore under Paragraph a, may also be applied to any ocean-going vessel or aircraft that has been ordered or the improvement of which has been let out prior to 1st January 1981, provided the investment is made prior to 1st January 1982.
10. If in the course of any given year ocean-going vessels or aircraft, to which the preceding paragraph was made to apply, are disposed of, eight per cent of the proceeds shall be added to the profits of both that year and that of the next following year. Addition of the taxable profit shall only be applied if the vessel or aircraft is disposed off within ten years from the year in which the investment was made.
11. At the determination of the annual profit a reserve may be put aside to evenly spread costs, expenses and charges and to cover any risks, which, are ordinarily insured but were not insured, provided the said costs, expenses and charges and risks relate to ocean-going vessels and aircraft.
12. In the event that the entity has received any compensation for the loss of or damage to any assets as referred to in this Article, in excess of the fiscal book value respectively of such lost assets or of damaged parts of such assets, the excess amount may be reserved, if and as long as replacement of repair is contemplated, until such replacement or repair has been effected and the entity starts writing-off on the costs of replacement or repair.

The accelerated depreciation as referred to in paragraph 8 of this Article shall be reduced by the amount to be written off on the replacement and costs of repairs. Unless the replacement or repair should take more time, the reserve shall be liquidated and its balance shall be transferred to the profit and loss account in the fifth calendar year subsequent to the year in which the reserve has been created.
13. a. Notwithstanding the provisions of Article 10, any loss incurred for any financial year, applying the rules in the determination of profits (including the rules laid down in Paragraphs 8 to 11, inclusive, of this present Article), shall be carried forward to the six following years, starting with the first subsequent year.
b. Losses incurred in the course of the entity's initial six fiscal years shall be carried forward as set forth under letter a of this Paragraph 13 however without the six years' limitation.

The present Article 9A is perhaps the most modern portion of the law. Modern, because it takes into account the economic realities of the shipping and airline industries. The Article grasps the competitive and cyclical nature of the industry, the risks of the sea for the seamen and shipowners. Thus, the law does not only speak of the taxation, it also deals with matters of registration and inspection of vessels.

This article provides for the following fiscal incentives:

a. Reduced taxation.
b. Investment allowance.
c. Accelerated depreciation.
d. Deductibility of reserves set aside to spread and equalize costs; replacement of depreciable assets and insurance.
e. Unlimited time for loss-carry-forward for losses sustained for the first six years, with subsequent losses carried forward for a six year period.

The advantages of this Article may be availed of by shipping or airline corporations and partnerships established under the laws of the Netherlands Antilles. For companies engaged in transportation rather than chartering, the day-to-day management must be conducted within the Netherlands Antilles.

Reduced Taxation

This article provides for taxation of the worldwide income of the shipping or airline company or partnership but the rate applied to 80% of the taxable income is one-tenth of the normal taxation rate and the rate applied on the balance is the full rate. The effective range of taxation is from 7.7% for the first NAf 100,000.– and 9.6% for any amount in excess. However, with all the other fiscal facilities offered by this article, the resulting effective rates may further be reduced.

Investment Allowance

A total of 16% of the amount of any contractual obligation of the taxable entity for the acquisition or improvement of a vessel or aircraft may be deducted from the taxable income of the said entity, 8% on the first year and the other 8% on the subsequent year.

The contractual obligation may be entered into between related parties and the Article does not provide for a minimum investment. However, if the vessel or aircraft is sold within 10 years from the fiscal year during which the investment allowance is taken, this article provides for a recapture of the investment allowance deduction. 8% of the transfer price of the vessel or aircraft shall be added to the taxable income of the transfer on the fiscal year when the transfer is made and the same amount is added to the subsequent fiscal year. However, if the vessel or aircraft is sold for an amount in excess of its acquisition price, the Inspector of Taxes of the Netherlands Antilles has ruled that the investment allowance recaptured will be determined on the basis of its original acquisition price instead of the higher selling price.

Accelerated Depreciation

As discussed under Article 5 of the present law, the norm used for depreciating assets in the Netherlands Antilles is simply 'normal and acceptable commercial practice'. This article is an exception to the provisions of Article 5. The acquisition price and/or the costs incurred to repair or improve the vessel or aircraft may be taken as the value of the asset. Vessels or aircraft previously owned and depreciated may further be depreciated based on the acquisition price of the asset. 'Accordingly, the acquisition cost of a vessel or aircraft should be divided into a two thirds and a one third part. With respect to each part the normal depreciation should be determined in accordance with the depreciation method chosen, before taking all or part of the accelerated depreciation on the third part. As a result, the depreciable amount each year may vary between two limits in such a way that the total amount which has been depreciated at the end of the fiscal year is subject to a maximum onethird of the acquisition price plus the total normal depreciation of the whole acquisition cost.' [13] The present article guarantees this accelerated depreciation with respect to ocean going vessels and aircraft ordered prior to the 1st of January, 1981, provided they are acquired prior to the 1st of January, 1982. In all likelihood the guarantees and facilities granted under this article will be extended again as the present article is already an extention of the previous expiration date of 1971.

Deductibility of Reserves Created for Replacement, Insurance and Reserves Set Aside to Spread and Equalize Costs, Expenses and Charges

Contrary to the provisions of Article 6 of the present law, the creation before tax, of a reserve fund is allowed under this present article. In addition to the ordinary and accelerated depreciation which by its nature is supposed to provide for the replacement of the depreciable

13. Smeets, G.C.A., Special Provisions for the Taxation of Netherlands Antilles Shipping and Aviation Companies, Bulletin of the International Bureau of Fiscal Documentation, Vol. XXVI, No. 8, August, 1972.

asset, an additional reserve was allowed, referred to as the 'replacement reserve' through the amendment of the law in 1970. This replacement reserve may be created not only to cover the replacement of the asset but also to cover costs of repair in case of damage to the vessel or aircraft. In addition, if normal insurable risks would, in practice, have been insured, but the corporation or partnership opted to create its own insurance reserve, said reserve is deductible. Finally, reserves may be created to spread over a number of years the costs and charges of the corporation or partnership in so far as the said costs and charges relate to the operation of the vessel or aircraft. However, replacement reserves if unused should be added back to taxable income in the fifth year.

In case of a voluntary sale of an aircraft or vessel, the Inspector may grant through a Tax Ruling that the Profits made on the sale of the asset may be placed on reserve for the acquisition of another vessel or aircraft, provided, the reserve is used as a write-off for the first year of operation of the newly acquired vessel or aircraft.

Carry Forward of Losses

Under present law, losses incurred by a taxable entity may be carried forward to a maximum of five years. This article allows a loss carry forward incurred for the first six years of operation for an unlimited number of years. Losses incurred on the seventh year and onwards, may be carried forward for six years. 'Losses include book losses created by application of the acclerated depreciation and the investment allowance.'[14]

Herein below is a hypothetical example of some of the taxation advantages offered by the present article.

An Antillean Shipping Company, which purchases a ship for US $15,000,000 may have the following deductions for the first 3 years.

1st year:	
a. Accelerated depreciation 33 1/3%	$ 5,000,000
b. Normal depreciation (during 15 years, salvage value $ 250,000	$ 650,000
c. Insurance reserve (Note 1)	$ 120,000
d. Maintenance reserve (Note 2) applicable in the 5th year	$ 150,000
e. Investment allowance 8%	$ 1,200,000
	$ 7,120,000

14. See note 13.

2nd year:	
a. Normal depreciation	$ 650,000
b. Insurance reserve	$ 120,000
c. Maintenance reserve	$ 150,000
d. Investment allowance 8%	$ 1,200,000
	$ 2,120,000

3rd year:	
a. Normal depreciation	$ 650,000
b. Insurance reserve	$ 120,000
c. Maintenance reserve	$ 150,000
	$ 920,000

Notes

(1) The contribution to the insurance reserve has to cease when the reserved amount has no relation to the value of the ship. The yearly contribution must be more or less equal to the normal insurance premium.

(2) The annual contribution is based on the estimated amount which is required after 5 years for maintenance.

With allowable expenses as shown in the foregoing hypothetical example, the Antillean shipping company may have a positive cash flow but will, in the ordinary course of business, register a loss due to the liberal allowances for depreciation and reserves. Since the losses of the first six years may be carried forward for an unlimited period of time, the Antillean shipping company will probably be successful in sheltering its profits from taxation for several years.

The registration of vessels in the Netherlands Antilles is governed by Maritime Law as well as the Code of Commerce of the Netherlands Antilles.

Article 10: Loss Carry Forward

When applying the rules for the determination of profit should a loss in any year result, said loss shall be carried forward to offset any profits in the succeeding five years, commencing with the first succeeding year.

Five years is the maximum time a loss may be carried forward as a deduction to profits made in the succeeding year.

In the Netherlands Antilles since there are different taxation rates applicable to profits derived from different activities of an entity, losses incurred in one specific activity with a specific taxation rate applicable, may not be carried forward as a deduction to taxable income of a different activity with a different taxation rate. Thus, losses incurred where the taxation rate is one-tenth the normal rate cannot be carried forward as a deduction to taxable income as a result of activities wherein the applicable taxation rate is the normal rate as provided for under Article 15.

However, for Antillean entities with branch profits derived from without the Netherlands Antilles different rules of loss-carry-forward apply as will be discussed later in this book.

Article 11: Dividend Tax Exemption

1. No tax shall be levied on the net income derived from a share of the profit, including distributions from any surplus of any trade or business, or any subdivision thereof in respect of which no deduction is allowed by virtue of the provisions of Article 6, paragraph 2 letter e, of:

a. corporations, associations, companies or foundations, referred to in Article 1, paragraph 1, letters a and b, other than corporations as referred to in Article 8A, Article 14 or Article 14A, unless the beneficiary is itself a corporation as referred in Article 8A, Article 14 or Article 14A.

b. entities as referred to in Article 1, paragraph 1, letter c which, in the year the profit distribution was earned, derived at least nine/tenths of its total profit from the Netherlands Antilles. In either case the amounts distributed on the shares or other instruments of participation have not been deducted from the book value of such shares or participations.

2. For the application of the preceding paragraph, the total profits of entities as referred to in Article 1, paragraph 1 letter c, shall be determined in accordance with the provisions of Articles 4 to 7 inclusive.

3. No tax shall moreover be levied on interest and other considerations received from corporations, companies, associations or foundations or other entities, insofar as such interest or other considerations are not deductible from taxable income pursuant to the provisions of Article 6, paragraph 2, letter c, insofar as the interest and other payments are indirectly for the account of the recipient of said interest or other forms of payments. The corporations referred to in this paragraph do not include corporations referred to in Article 8A, Article 14 or Article 14A, unless the recipient entity itself is a corporation referred to in Article 8A, Article 14A.

This article grants Antillean domiciled entities exemption from double Antillean profit taxation subject to certain conditions. The general principle is that expenses not deductible from the taxable income of the payor-entity are not taxable in the hands of the payee-entity.

The conditions referred to above may best be illustrated by the following:

1. Company A and Company B are both Netherlands Antilles Companies not enjoying special tax treatment as granted by Articles 8A, 14 and 14A of the present law ('on shore companies'). A is a shareholder of B. Dividend paid by B to A is not taxable income in the hands of A.
2. A is a company enjoying special tax treatment as granted by Articles 8A, 14 and 14A of the present law, ('off shore company'). Dividend paid by B, an 'on shore company', to A is free of tax in the hands of A.
3. Company A and Company B are both 'off shore companies'. A is a shareholder of B. Dividend paid by B to A is free of tax in the hands of A.
4. Company A is an 'on shore company' which holds shares of Company B, an 'off shore company'. Dividend paid by B to A is fully taxable in the hands of A. (The foregoing illustrations should not be read as a definition of the concept of 'off shore company'. Later on we shall see that the concept of 'off shore company' is broader than simply a company enjoying taxation advantages granted under Articles 8A, 14 or 14A.)

It should be noted that the exemption from double Antillean taxation of entities in the Netherlands Antilles does not, in practice, fully exempt the dividend received from profit taxation. In several cases, the Court has supported the Inspector of Taxes in his position that if the payee of the dividend itself has a loss, the dividend received shall be compensated fully against the loss and thus diminish if not altogether eliminate said loss for the current fiscal year or its carry forward for the subsequent fiscal years.

The same foregoing illustrations will apply if the payor-entity is a non-Netherlands Antilles entity but derived 90% of the income which it is distributing from within the Netherlands Antilles.

The same foregoing illustrations will apply for interest and other forms of payment made by an entity to its shareholders or members. However, it should be emphasized that the amount of interest paid should be a non-deductible item from the Payor's taxable income as provided for under Article 6, paragraph 2 letter c. There may be situa-

15. For a short description in English, see Tax Facilities for Netherlands Antillean Limited Liability Companies Operating Shipping or Air Services, published by the Cabinet of the Minister Plenepotentiary of The Netherlands Antilles, The Hague, undated.

tions wherein interest paid by a subsidiary to its parent is a deductible item from its taxable income. For example, a Netherlands Antilles off shore company lends money to a subsidiary company which is also a Netherlands Antilles Company but said subsidiary is doing realty business in the USA through a permanent establishment. By virtue of Article 5 of the Tax Convention between the Netherlands and the USA as extended to the Netherlands Antilles, the subsidiary realty company is only taxable in the USA. However, since the interest paid by said subsidiary is a deductible item to its taxable income in the USA, the interest received by the lender-parent company is taxable under Article 14 of the present law. We will see that such interest income is taxable at the low rate of 2.4-3% if the lender-parent company enjoys special tax treatment under Articles 8A, 14 or 14A of the present law.

Article 12: Foreign Source Income

1. No tax shall be levied on the net income of any corporation, association, company or foundation referred to in Article 1, paragraph 1 letters a and b derived from sources within The Netherlands or Surinam (since the 25th of November, 1975, Surinam no longer forms a part of the Kingdom of The Netherlands, and therefore this provision no longer applies to Surinam) arising from any trade or business carried on through a permanent establishment or from real property situated therein (including right attached to such real property), provided a tax in any shape or form on profits is levied on the trade or business or on real property in such country. Insofar as profit derived from abroad (i.e. outside the Kingdom of The Netherlands) is concerned, a tax shall be levied on such profits at one/tenth of the normal rates as referred to in Article 15.
2. For the application of the first paragraph, the profits derived from within the Kingdom of The Netherlands or abroad, (i.e. outside the Kingdom of The Netherlands) shall be determined in accordance with Articles 4 to 7 inclusive. With respect to the insurance business, the profits shall be determined in accordance with the principles contained in Article 8 paragraphs 5 and 6.

This Article exempts or reduces the taxation on the profit of Antillean entities doing business without the Netherlands Antilles through a permanent establishment.

For a clearer understanding of 'permanent establishment', the discussion under Article 1 may help in the clarification of the concept which the present law does not define.

BRANCH LOSS CARRY FORWARD

A distinction is made as to profits derived from The Netherlands and profits derived from other countries. Profits derived from The Netherlands are exempt from tax and those derived from elsewhere are taxed at one-tenth of the normal tates. The article however, requires that a tax, constituting a certain given percentage of the profits, should be levied on the income of the Antillean entity doing business through a permanent establishment abroad. The law only requires that there is a tax in whatever shape or form, it does not require that such a tax be actually imposed. Thus, an Antillean entity which is doing business in a country which offers what often is referred to as a 'tax holiday' or a tax exemption may not actually pay any tax but if the country has some form of profit taxation, then the Antillean Company will only pay one/tenth of the normal rates in the Netherlands Antilles.

The present article does not always apply to Antillean entities doing business in a country with a Tax Convention on Double Taxation with The Netherlands Antilles. The taxation imposed herein may sometimes give way to the provisions of a Treaty, e.g. the UK.

For the computation of profits of the Antillean entity with a permanent establishment abroad, the provisions of the present law shall be made to apply and not the law of the country where the Antillean entity is doing business. Thus, an expense may be deductible item to taxable income in another jurisdiction but if not deductible in the Netherlands Antilles, the deduction will be added back to taxable income of the Antillean entity.

When consolidating the financial statements of Antillean entities with a branch abroad doing business therein through a permanent establishment, the losses of the branch (note that if it were profits these would be taxed at the lower rates) if used to offset the profits made within, and taxable at full rates in, the Netherlands Antilles, should be fully recompensated at full rates in the subsequent fiscal years before the profits of the branch can enjoy taxation at lower rates.

To illustrate:
An Antillean Company has a branch in Guatemala.

Year	*Antillean Company*	*Guatemala Branch*	*Taxable Income*	*Rate*
First	Profit 1,000,000	(Loss) 200,000	800,000	Full
Second	Profit 900,000	Profit 100,000	1,000,000	Full
Third	Profit 850,000	Profit 150,000	950,000	Full
			50,000	Low
Fourth	Profit 800,000	Profit 150,000	800,000	Full
			150,000	Low

Article 13: Qualified Participation

1. Without prejudice to the provisions of Article 11, no tax shall be levied on the net income received by a corporation, association, company or foundation referred to in Article 1, Paragraph 1, letters a and b other than a corporation referred to under Article 14 Paragraph 1 or in Article 14A Paragraph 1, and a corporation to which Article 14 Paragraph 12 or Article 14A Paragraph 3 is applicable on distributions of profits of any entity established without the Netherlands Antilles (the term entity includes all companies or associations the capital of which is wholly or partly divided into shares) provided that the entity is situated in a country where a tax on profits is levied in whatever form for the benefit of such country. Where the entity is situated within The Netherlands or Surinam, no tax shall be levied as herein above-mentioned provided, however, if the entity is situated without the Kingdom of The Netherlands, a taxation rate of one tenth of the normal rates referred to in Article 15 shall be applied.
2. The provisions of Paragraph 1 of this article shall only apply to any holder of a share of stock or an instrument of participation provided that the shareholding or the participation represents a 'qualified participation' and the amount distributed is not deducted from the book value of such share of stock or instrument of participation.
3. The term 'qualified participation' shall be understood to mean the possession of shares of stock or instruments of participation held in pursuit of the ordinary course of business or the acquisition of which was made for the general interest. Whenever the holding of the shares of stock or the instrument of participation represents at least one tenth of the nominal paid-in capital of the entity distributing its profits, a 'qualified participation' shall always be deemed to exist.

This article is similar although not identical in scope to Article 11. It grants exemption from double taxation subject to certain conditions.

Exemption applies to entities in the Netherlands Antilles which do not enjoy a special tax treatment by falling within the definition in the first paragraphs of Articles 14 and 14A, provided, that the entity is not covered by the provisions of the last paragraph of Article 14 or the third paragraph of Article 14A. We shall see in the discussion under the next two articles that the benefits provided for by the present article are not granted to corporations often referred to as 'off shore companies'.

Antillean resident companies receiving dividends from an entity established and doing business without the Netherlands Antilles may be exempted from taxation on said dividends or may be liable for a lower rate of taxation. The dividend is tax-exempt if the payor-entity is established and doing business in the Netherlands and if established elsewhere, the Antillean entity is liable to a tax at the rate of one tenth of the normal rate as provided for in Article 15. This exemption or lower rate privilege will only apply provided:

1. The Antillean Payee of the dividend holds a 'qualified participation' in the payor-entity.
2. In the country where the payor-entity is established and doing business, there is a tax, constituting a certain given percentage of the profits, imposable for the benefit of the situs-country.

The present article cites two instances wherein a 'qualified participation' may be deemed to exist:

1. The participation of the Antillean payee in the foreign payor (as shareholder or holder of any profit sharing instrument) was made in pursuit of its ordinary course of trade and business.

2. The participation by the Antillean payee was made for the 'general interest'.

Participation made in the normal course of business can only be presumed if there exists an 'inseparable connection'[16] between the payee and the payor of the dividend. For example, where an Antillean company formed a wholly owned subsidiary abroad for the manufacture of goods but due to nationalisation requirements, the Antillean company's participation had to be reduced to less than 10% of the company abroad but the former subsidiary could not go on manufacturing without the input from its former parent, the Antillean company; it is submitted, has an inseparable connection and therefore a qualified participation for the exemption of dividend income remains. An investment made by manufacturing company however, of its surplus or reserve funds cannot be considered made in the normal course of business 'neither can a holding of a few listed shares in a stock exchange of a large corporation be characterized[17] as made in the normal course of business.

A participation made for the general interest has been interpreted [18] as a participation made at the urging of or on the insistence by the government. A 'qualified participation' will always be deemed to exist if the Payee of the dividend holds at least ten percent of the 'Nominal paid up capital' of the Payor entity. The 'nominal paid-up capital' as used in the third paragraph of the present article has been interpreted to mean the total equity capital of the payor-entity.

16. De Klerck and Muller, p. 352.
17. See note 16.
18. See note 16.

The tax exemption or the lower taxation privilege provided for herein only applies to dividend income and not to interest.

Finally, it should be noted that the benefits provided for by Article 13 may be waived by the Payee, e.g. if required in order to avail of the benefits of certain treaty arrangements of the Netherlands Antilles e.g. Treaty with the USA.

On-Shore Companies

Before we examine a different genre of taxation in the Netherlands Antilles applicable to off shore companies which are primarily governed by Articles 14, 14A and 8A, it will be necessary to clearly outline the taxation rates applicable to on-shore companies.

Contrary to popular belief, on-shore companies may avail of the special taxation rate of one/tenth the full rate provided for under Article 15 of the present law. The essential difference between the application of the rates to off-shore companies and on-shore companies is in the case of the latter the Island's surtax is applied on top of the rates provided for under Article 15, may it be the one/tenth rate or the full rate.

The applicable taxation rates for one-shore companies are as follows:

0% – 2% – 3.1% to 3.9% – 31.05% to 39.1%.

The 2% rate applies to Free Zone companies and the 3.1% to 3.9% are the one/tenth rates of the full rates inclusive the surtax. Generally, for the first NAf. 40,000 of taxable income, 3.1% or 31.05% is applicable depending on whether the one/tenth or the full rate is applicable. For amounts over NAf. 100,000 but under NAf. 1,000,000 rates applicable are 3.8% or 37.95% again depending on whether the one/tenth or the full rate is applicable. Finally, for amounts in excess of NAf. 1,000,000 the rates could either be 3.9% or 39.1%. Article 15 provides the detailed scale of taxation.

In the following pages are flow-charts which outline the applicable taxation rates on on-shore-companies.

Hereinbelow are descriptions of some of the terms used in the flowchart.

Passive Income: Refers to investment income such as dividends, interest, royalty, including rent of tangible personalty and capital gain. Dividend includes income derived from profit certificates or 'jouissance' shares. Rentals derived from the exhibition of motion pictures or industrial, commercial and scientific equipment are classified as passive income.

Active Income: Refers to business profits the generation of which generally requires a greater or more active participation by the taxable entity than is normally required in the generation of passive income.

N.B. The foregoing are generic descriptions rather than clear definitions. The facts of a given situation may alter the general classification of income from passive to active and vice versa. The law as we shall see under Articles 14 and 14A describes the purpose of the taxable entity rather than its income in order to determine the applicable taxation rate. It does not define the income produced but describes the producer of the income.

Free Zone Company: A corporation incorporated within or without the Netherlands Antilles which has complied with all the requirements of the law and pursuant to said law has been granted the permit to operate within the Free Zone.

Investment made in the normal course of business: See commentary under Article 13.

Taxation Rates of On-Shore Companies in the Netherlands Antilles

Chart 1

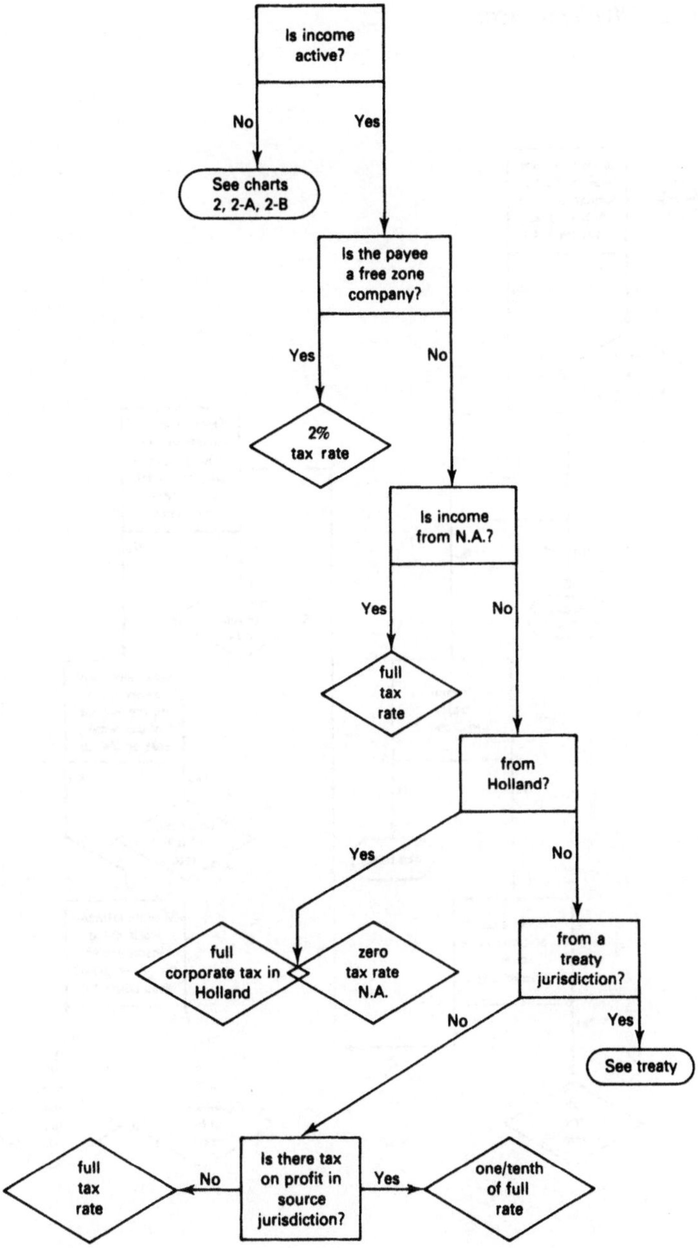

Taxation Rates of On-Shore Companies in the Netherlands Antilles – Passive Income

N.B. Capital Gain when realized is always taxable.

Chart 2: Dividend Income

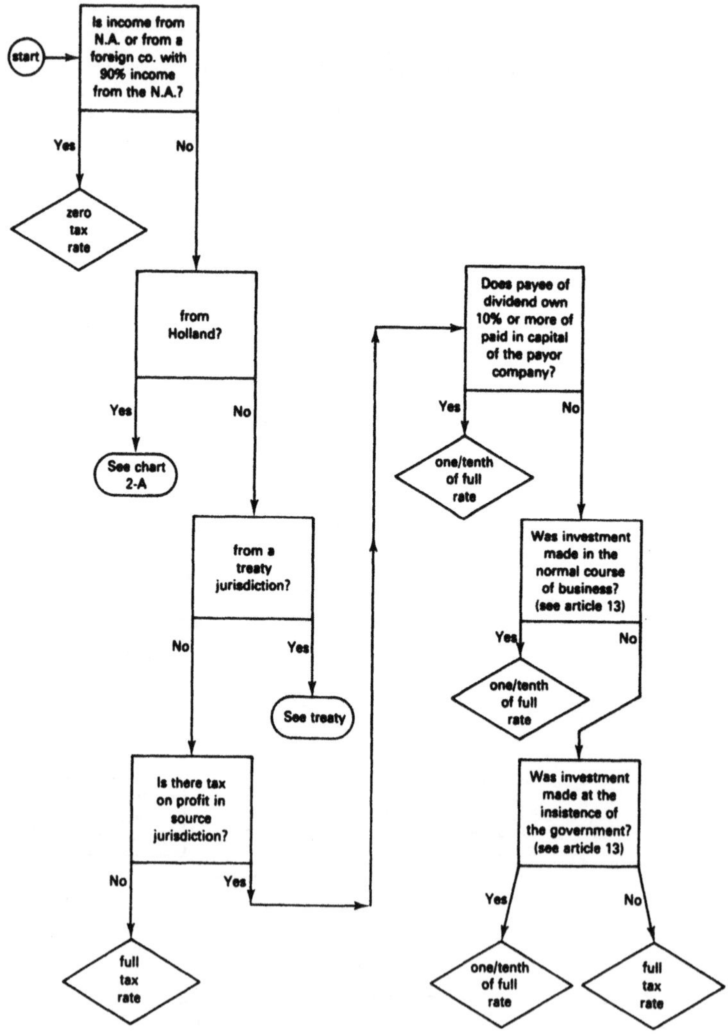

Taxation Rates of On-Shore Companies in the Netherlands Antilles – Passive Income

Chart 2A: Dividend Income
the Netherlands

Chart 2B: Interest Income World-wide

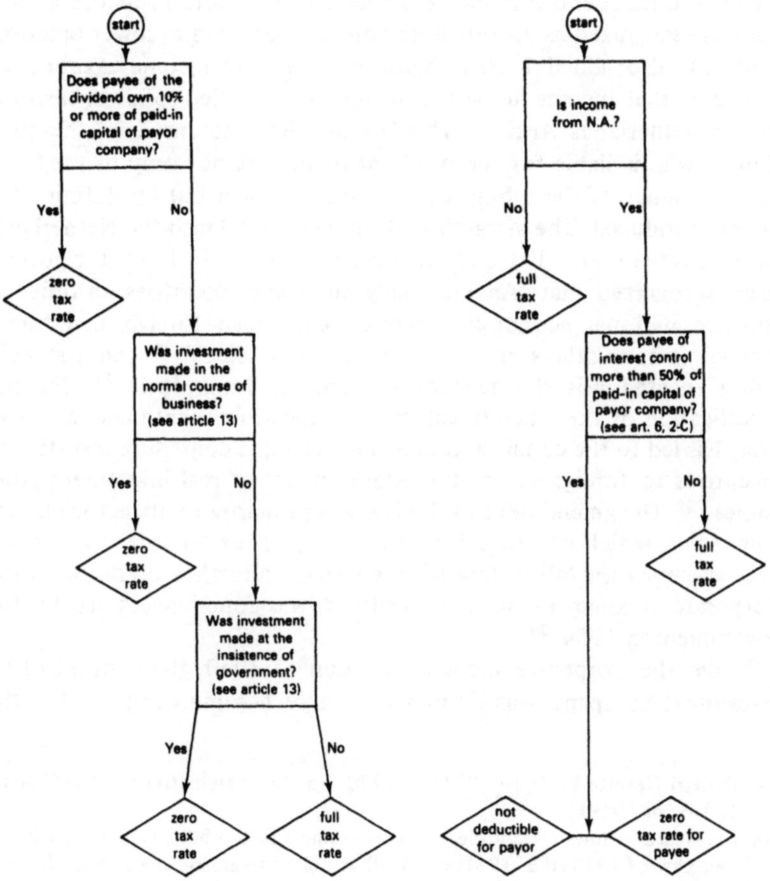

Off-Shore Companies

The principal provisions of the law which govern the taxation, and to a degree, the operation of off-shore companies are Articles 14, 14A and Article 8A of the present law. The addition and alteration of these articles, however, necesitated the amendment of other articles and thus, we have seen under several articles, references are made to the above three principal articles. The Guaranty Ordinance on Profit Taxation of 1969 [19] supplemented the present law both in the substantive and formal requirements for the recognition of off-shore companies.

The Guaranty Ordinance of 1969 added the procedural or formal requirement of a foreign exchange license from the Bank of the Netherlands Antilles (Central Bank) as a substantive condition before a company is recognized as an off-shore company entitled to lower taxation. This law also added a new factor in corporate income taxation by providing that income derived from abroad is entitled to lower taxation in the Netherlands Antilles. This law of 1969 also answered the question of who is liable for the payment of the tax not only in the traditional manner of describing the income producer but by defining the income-produced. The attraction of foreign capital into the Netherlands Antilles is the raison d'etre of off-shore companies. In 1951, the government recognized that 'An increasing number of countries, in order to enhance national economic interests, encourage foreign investment through, among others, favourable taxation measures'. [20] The first legislation enacted was the Law of the 2nd of June, 1951. [21] 'Further investigation of the amendment made in the afore-mentioned law however, has led to the conclusion that these changes constitute insufficient incentives to foreigners for the establishment of real investment companies.' [22] The amendment to the law was primarily to attract insurance companies, which was found unsatisfactory. Thus, in order to accomodate and meet the 'objections of foreigners ... a further alteration of the Corporate Income Taxation of 1940' [23] was found necessary by the government in 1954. [24]

Under the Corporate Income Taxation of 1940, the concept of an investment company was limited to a pure holding company but the

19. Official Gazette 1970, No. 93 (P.B. 1970, No. 93) (hereinafter cited as Guaranty Law of 1969).
20. Explanatory notes ('Memorie van Toelichting') to the bill to amend the Profit Tax Law of 1940 (P.B. 1951, No. 150) as well as to amend the Law on Income Taxation 1943 (P.B. 1942, No. 247), Staten van de Nederlandse Antillen 1952-1953-39, No. 3, page 1 (hereinafter cited as MvT 1952-53).
21. Official Gazette, 1951, No. 150 (P.B. 1951, No. 150).
22. MvT 1952-53, page 1.
23. See note 22.
24. Official Gazette, 1955, No. 140 (P.B. 1955, No. 140).

amendment in 1954 adopted a 'broader point of view of holding companies'.[25] Unlike other jurisdictions where a sharp delineation is made between investment companies and active income producing companies, the amendment in 1954 liberalized the interpretation of investment companies and granted the Inspectorate of Taxes the discretion to impose one set of taxation rates for investment income and another for business and commercial profits of the same company. The legislature explained that 'although the proposed arrangement is meant, in principle, to apply to corporations which operate exclusively as investment or holding company, it may occur that, a company is engaged in investment activities as well as other activities. Thus, in order to prevent inequity, it appears desirable to grant the Inspector the authority, when requested by the taxpayer, to make a separate assessment of the capital gain of the investment company'.[26]

This rather broad interpretation of the concept of investment company gave rise to a different type of financial reporting, in so far as taxation is concerned in the Netherlands Antilles. 'Income of the investment company (according to the broad interpretation of Article 12, Paragraph 1 and the "other activity" are kept strictly separate.'[27] The legislators cautioned that 'utmost care must be taken that stockholdings which are not directly connected with investment activity ...' are not imputed to this investment company, e.g. stockholdings that are only held as temporary investment of cash belonging to the 'other activity' are not to be inputed to such an 'investment company'.[28]

The law or present jurisprudence does not give a clear definition of an off-shore. Not only must one look into the law on Corporate Income Taxation of 1940, but as stated above, other laws and regulations must be examined to determine whether a company is off-shore and the rate of taxation for a specific income derived from a specific activity. Specific rules for the allocation of expenses and the carry forward of losses have been set out by rules and policies of the Inspector of Taxes and jurisprudence as we have seen under Articles 11 and 12, which while specifically discussed under on-shore companies also applies to off-shore companies.

However, there are four distinctive elements which must concur before a company may be considered an off-shore company, under Articles 8A, 14 and 14A.

1. The Company must be a corporation (an n.v.).[29]

25. MvT 1952-53, page 1.
26. MvT 1952-53, page 2.
27. MvT 1952-53, page 3.
28. MvT 1952-53, page 4.
29. Article 14, par. 1, Profit Tax Law of 1940 as amended (hereinafter cited as Winstbelasting 1940).

2. The shareholders must be non-residents of the Netherlands Antilles. [30]
3. The corporation must have been granted a Foreign Exchange License by the Bank of the Netherlands Antilles. [31]
4. The income of the corporation must be derived from without the Netherlands Antilles, except for interest income derived from local banks within the Netherlands Antilles, provided, however, the corporation is not engaged in trade or business in the Netherlands Antilles through a permanent establishment. [32]

Due to the importance, complexity and length of the following Article 14, it will be discussed in several parts.

Article 14: Off-Shore Companies

1. a. To corporations referred to under Article 1, Paragraph 1 under letter a, the object of which is exclusively or almost exclusively to invest its assets in securities, such as shares and other evidences of participations, bonds and other interest bearing claims on debt under whatever name and in whatever form, shall be applied, the provisions of paragraph 3 up to and including paragraph 11.

b. The provisions under letter a hereof, shall not be made to apply to a corporation the object of which is as set forth under letter a, if said corporation notifies the Inspector, in writing, before the end of its fiscal year that the provisions of this article shall be made inapplicable to it.

c. The term 'securities' as referred to under letter a shall not include, bills of exchange, promissory notes, acceptances and other claims on debts arising out of commercial or credit transactions within the Netherlands Antilles, as well as claims on debts which, in so far as the principal is concerned, are secured by mortgage on real property situated within the Netherlands Antilles.

The amendment of the first paragraph of this article in 1963 [33] further expanded the coverage of the special lower taxation privilege of companies incorporated in the Netherlands Antilles. The article presently includes 'bonds and other interest bearing claims on debts under whatever name and in whatever form'.

30. Article 5, par. 4, Law on Income Taxation of 1943, as amended (hereinafter cited as Inkomstenbelasting 1943).
31. Article 3 under letter B, par. 2, Guaranty Law of 1969.
32. Article 3 under letters A and B, Guaranty Law of 1969.
33. Official Gazette, 1963, No. 23 (P.B. 1963, No. 23).

Prior to the amendment the privilege was confined to companies the object of which is the 'ownership, the possession, the management and alienation of securities in the widest sense of the word'. [34]

The term 'securities' is limited by the qualification made under letter C of the first paragraph of this article which excludes receivables arising out of commercial or credit transactions within the Netherlands Antilles. This exclusion was revised in 1969 [35] by the enactment of the law which classified 'interest enjoyed on credit balances with banking institutions situated within the Netherlands Antilles' [36] as entitled to the lower taxation privilege.

The article is not explicit about commercial or credit transactions between two Netherlands Antilles off-shore companies as it is explicit under Articles 4 or 11. However, by implication, the grant of a foreign exchange license to an off-shore company by the Bank of the Netherlands Antilles, the grantee of the license is considered as a non-resident. The Foreign Exchange Ordinance of 1940 [37] provides a definition as to who are to be considered as non-residents and 'In practice, this provision has been construed in such a way, as to include the so called off-shore companies'. [38]

As non-residents therefore, their transactions are deemed to have been entered into without the Netherlands Antilles, notwithstanding the fact that corporations are considered to be established within the Netherlands Antilles simply by the fact that they are incorporated under the laws of the Netherlands Antilles. [39] It should be noted, however, that both companies should be off-shore companies and not only one of the two. It should further be noted that notwithstanding the fact that both are off-shore companies, the transaction will not be entitled to a lower taxation privilege if the payment of the principal amount in the credit transaction is secured by real estate situated within the Netherlands Antilles.

The waiver of the lower taxation privilege provided for under letter b of Paragraph 1 of this article is very seldom availed of. Only under those circumstances wherein the applicable taxation rate is zero, e.g. certain types of dividend income from The Netherlands, will a taxable corporation notify the Inspector, in writing, of its desire not to be taxed at the low rate.

34. See Official Gazette 1960, No. 215 (P.B. 1960, No. 215).
35. Guaranty Law of 1969.
36. Article 3, letter B, Guaranty Law 1969.
37. Official Gazette, 1941, No. 136, (P.B. 1941, No. 136).
38. Bank van de Nederlandse Antillen, Quarterly Bulletin, 1975, vol. 3-4, p. 13.
39. Article 1, paragraph 2, Winstbelasting 1940.

2. In deviation of the provisions of Paragraph 1 under letter a, the provisions of this article shall not apply to a corporation, which has been subject to corporate income tax for a preceding fiscal year on a basis other than that provided for in this article, unless a request in writting is made with to Inspector of Taxes. The Inspector of Taxes will only grant such a request if the corporation concerned values its assets and liabilities, as referred to in paragraph 10, in its balance sheet as of the close of the fiscal year preceding the fiscal year to which the application of the provisions of this article is requested, at their market value.

3. In the event that the provisions of Paragraphs 3 through 11 of this article to a corporation pursuant to either Paragraph 1, under letter a of Paragraph 2 of this article, these provisions shall remain applicable until:

a. the objectives of the corporation cease to be in conformity with the requirements of the first paragraph under letter a, or
b. the corporation itself requests the Inspector of Taxes in writing, that the provisions in this article cease to apply and the Inspector of Taxes has granted such a request.

4. a. In a case as referred to in the preceding paragraph, under letter a, the assets and liabilities, as referred to in Paragraph 10, of the corporation concerned, shall be valued at their market value, in order to determine the profit of the corporation at the time that the objectives of the corporation should be regarded to have ceased to comply with the provisions of Paragraph 1 under letter a.

b. A request as referred to in the preceding paragraph under letter b will only be granted by the Inspector of Taxes if the assets and liabilities referred to in Paragraph 10, and appearing in the opening balance of the first fiscal year in respect of which the request is made, are appraised at their market value.

5. Requests as referred to in Paragraph 2 and Paragraph 3, under letter b will take effect only in respect of fiscal years, which have not yet started at the time that the requests are made, unless the Inspector at his discretion decides otherwise.

The provisions of Paragraphs 2 to 5 of the present article regulate the manner a company may opt to be taxed under this Article at one tenth the normal rate or to be subjected to taxation under other articles of the present law and vice versa.

The exercise of the option to be taxed under the provisions of this article can only be granted by the Inspector of Taxes, provided:

1. A request, in writing, is made;
2. The company re-values its assets and liabilities in its balance sheet at

market value as contemplated under paragraph 10 of the present article;

3. The objectives of the corporation fulfil the conditions as provided tor under Paragraph 1 under letter a hereof.

The exercise of this option when granted by the Inspector will result in the taxation of the unrealized and realized capital gains made by the company in the previous fiscal year.

A company taxed under this Article may revert and be subject of taxation under the provisions of other articles, either:

1. By operation of the law, i.e. when the company ceases to fulfil the requirements of Paragraph 1 hereof; or
2. At its own request, in writing, made to and granted by the Inspector of Taxes.

In either case, the assets and liabilities of the company must be revalued at market value either at the time it ceases to fulfil the requirements of paragraph 2 hereof or at the opening of the fiscal year in respect of which the request is made. As a consequence of this revaluation, the company will not be liable for taxation in respect of its capital gains realized or unrealized but it will still be subject to taxation under this article.

In general, the changes abovementioned shall take effect in the succeeding fiscal year unless the Inspector rules otherwise.

6. Without prejudice to the provisions of Article 11, the profit of a corporation as referred to in Paragraph 1 under letter a shall be subject to a corporate income tax at one tenth of the rate of Article 15 if and insofar as the profit consists of net amounts received as: income from securities, such as dividends (including liquidation-dividends) from shares and other participations and interest on bonds, or interest on other claims on debts, under any name and under whatever from yet to be mentioned.

7. a. The income mentioned in the foregoing paragraph includes original issue-discounts as well as interest included in amortization payments on claims on debts.

b. The income mentioned in the foregoing paragraph does not include interest (including discounts) derived from commercial papers and claims on debts as mentioned in Paragraph 1 under letter c.

Paragraph 6 by reference to Article 15 of the present law lays down the taxation rates applicable to companies with passive income. Paragraph 7 amplifies the coverage of the present article and at the same time reiterates the limitation imposed by Paragraph 1 under letter c.

Paragraph 6 is the general rule applicable to the lower taxation of passive income of companies. The exception to this rule is Article 11 which grants exemption from double Antillean taxation of companies. Thus, a liquidation dividend paid by a foreign subsidiary of an Antillean company is taxed at the low rate, while the liquidation dividend paid by an Antillean subsidiary to an Antillean parent is not taxed at all.

The 'claims on debts' provided for under Paragraph 6 includes mortgage interest income provided it originates from a non-treaty jurisdiction.

8. A distribution in stock shall be regarded as a dividend payment, if and insofar as the distribution is made out of the profits of the distributing entity and insofar as it is not evidenced that the shares have been or will be paid.

The writing up of shares shall be regarded as a distribution. The stock received will be appraised to arrive at the income as referred to under Paragraph 6 as follows:

a. If the distribution consists of shares in the capital stock of the distributing entity, the distribution shall be appraised at the par value of the shares distributed unless the amount transferred from the profits earned, or the retained earnings into the capital account in connection with the distribution of the shares differs from the par value, in which latter case, the amount so transferred shall prevail;
b. if the distribution consists of shares in the capital stock of an entity other than the distributing entity, the market value of the shares will prevail.

In deviation from the relevant provisions of this paragraph, a distribution as referred to under letter a shall not be regarded as dividend payment, if the shares in the capital stock of the distributing entity are quoted at a stock exchange or if they are otherwise publicly traded or offered.

The foregoing paragraph 8 specifically defines and provides for the taxation of stock dividends or what effectively is a stock dividend. A clear pronouncement and definition of what constitutes a stock dividend was found necessary under this article because this same article exempts taxation of capital gains, and in order to prevent avoidance of taxation by classifying dividend income as capital gain a clear definition of a stock dividend is necessary.

The following are considered as a stock dividend:

1. Any distribution of its own stock by a company to its shareholders wherein the latter have not or will not pay for the distribution;

2. Any distribution made by a company in the form of its own stock or any evidence of ownership thereof paid out of its profits or from its own retained earnings;
3. Any payment by the company on behalf of its shareholders which increases the shareholders participation in the capital account of the company, e.g. subscribed but not fully paid up shares when paid for by the company on behalf of the subscribers constitutes a stock dividend in the hands of the beneficiary of the payment.

The distribution of its own stock as a dividend by a company is appraised at its par value. However, if the amount transferred from profits or from retained earnings into the capital account is greater than the par value of the shares distributed as dividend, the amount so transferred to the capital account shall be the appraised value of the total dividend distribution. While Netherlands Antilles corporations always have shares with par, a distribution made by a foreign company of shares without par shall be appraised in the same manner.

A distribution in kind such as the distribution of the stock of companies other than the stock of the distributing entity itself shall be appraised at market value of the stocks so distributed.

The distribution itself must originate from the company rather than from a claim of the shareholder to the company. Thus, the exercise of an option or a stock warrant is considered as a capital gain rather than a stock dividend in the hands of the claimant-payee.

Any distribution made by an entity of its own stock to its shareholders shall not be taxable provided the shares of the distributing entity are listed in a stock exchange or otherwise publicly traded or offered. This exemption appears to be limited to a stock dividend of the entity itself and by omission excludes a dividend distribution in kind such as the distribution as dividend, the shares of other companies or entities.

> 9. If a corporation as referred to in Paragraph 1 under letter a has received income not referred to in Paragraph 6 – nor income as referred to in the next paragraph – the net amount of such income shall be taxed in accordance with the other provisions of this law.

This is a reiteration of the general rule that dividends, interest and also royalties (as referred to under Article 14A) received by a corporation meeting the requirements of this Article and other pertinent laws and regulations as we have seen earlier, are taxed at one tenth the rates provided for under Article 15, and capital gain, realized or unrealized, is not taxed at all. All other types of income may be taxed at the full rate or may still be at the low rate, depending on the source of the income, as we have seen under Article 12.

> 10. The profit of a corporation as referred to in the first paragraph under letter a does not include benefits derived from a *change in value*, or *the alienation of assets*, as referred to in Paragraph 6. The benefits derived from a change in value, or the alienation of non-interest bearing claims on debts, credit balance, as well as debts of the taxpayer, shall not be regarded as profit either.

This is a specific paragraph which exempts from taxation the income of companies derived from the change of value or the alienation of an asset, i.e. capital gain. The word 'benefit' as used in this paragraph should be interpreted in its arithmetical significance indicating both its positive and negative aspects and not in its popular significance indicating an advantage. With this as a premise, we must conclude that while capital gain is not taxable, the consequence is that capital loss is not deductible.

> 11. a. In order to arrive at the net amount of profit, as referred to in Paragraph 6, the income referred to in the said paragraph shall be decreased by an amount of reasonable expenses related to that income.
>
> b. The expenses referred to under letter a do not include interest on funds borrowed, unless such interest is due to a bank or a similar institution, which makes its business by lending funds to entities as referred to in Paragraph 1 under letter a. However, the provisions of Article 6, Paragraph 2, under letter c remain applicable.
>
> c. Insofar as the expenses referred to under letter a are not solely related to the acquisition of income, as referred to in Paragraph 6, but also relate to the purchase and sale of an earning asset, a pro-rated part of those expenses shall be attributed to the benefits as referred to in the foregoing paragraph; however, only and insofar as such benefits for the annual accounting period concerned are positive and have been realized.

The gross income of a company may be reduced by reasonable expenses incurred for the acquisition of such gross income. A reasonable expense shall be measured by the facts of each case following the general guidelines of good and acceptable commercial practice.

Interest as an expense is only deductible if payable to a bank or a similar institution. E.g. Interest payable to a broker is considered as payable to a 'similar institution.'[40] However, interest payable to a bank which controls directly or indirectly more than 50% of the stock of the payor corporation, as defined under Article 6 Paragraph 2 under letter c, is not deductible.[41]

The clearest manner to show the computation of a corporation's taxable income, specifically, the proration of expenses referred to under letter C of this paragraph is through an illustration using as a basis the following hypothetical Profit and Loss Account.

Income		*Expenses*	
Dividend (Non-Treaty)	4,000	Organization (Amortized 5 years)	1,000
Interest on Eurobonds	6,000	Management Fee	3,000
Royalties (Non-Treaty)	3,000	Interest: Loan from Bank	1,700
Gain on Sale of Securities	10,000	Margin account with broker	1,500
		Loan from shareholders	1,500
		Commissions	1,000
		Taxes and transfer fees	1,000
		Acquisition cost of patent amortized over 10 years	2,500
			13,200
		Profit (Loss)	9,800
	23,000		23,000

In computing the tax based on the foregoing Profit and Loss Account we are reproducing two pages of a corporate income Tax Return used in the Netherlands Antilles to illustrate the computation of the Tax. (See 'Return A' on pages 56 and 57.)

Using a similar but not identical Profit and Loss Account but assuming that the Dividend and Royalties are derived from the United States and the company avails of the Treaty benefits and to illustrate the treatment of capital losses, vis-à-vis, expenses, also assume, there is a 10,000 capital loss, the computation will be as shown in 'Return B' on pages 58 and 59.

40. As at 1 January, 1975, the Inspector of Taxes has made a General Ruling that interest payable to a broker which is a member of the National Association of Securities dealers in the U.S. is deductible.

41. The Inspector may at his discretion grant a ruling which in effect allows a deduction if the circumstances of the given situation could be seen as and therefore considered an 'arms length transaction'.

Return A

11. Division of Profit

	A Not taxable	B Subject to 1/10 of the rate	C Subject to 15% rate	D Subject to full rate
12. Income				
a. Securities				
1. not taxable (capital gains, etc.)	$ 10,000			
2. taxable		$ 4,000		
b. Interest		$ 6,000		
c. Royalties		$ 3,000		
d. Income/compensations art. 14A not being royalties				
e. Taxable income not mentioned under heading 12a through 12d				
f. Total				
g.	$ 10,000	$13,000		
h. Deduction of costs excluding profit tax paid (in case of interest paid indicate entity to which paid in heading no. 20) (Total costs:. $ 9,200 (a))	" 4,000	" 5,200		
Specify computation of allocation of costs under heading no. 20				
i. Profit	$ 6,000	$ 7,800		
Article 11(1)				
Article 11(1)				
13. Correction: Profit received share of profit of:				
a. Corporations, societies, companies or foundations as meant in sub paragraph a and b of paragraph 1 of article 1				
b. Entities as meant in sub paragraph .. of paragraph 1 of article 1 which derived at least 9/10 of the entire profit in the N.A. during the year to which the distributed profit applies				
Give specification under heading no. 20				
Article 11(3)				
14. Correction: Profit derived as interest on loans and/or compensation for the use or consumption of goods made available in whatever form to an entity meant in paragraph 1 of article 1 to which capital the body for which the return is filed is entitled.				
Give specification under heading no. 20				
Article 12(1)				

15. Correction: Profit derived from business conducted through a permanent establishment outside the N.A. or from real estate located outside the N.A. and which are subject to tax on profit: a. of business or real estate in The Netherlands or Surinam b. of business or real estate elsewhere Give specification under heading no. 20				
16. Correction				
	$ 6,000	$ 7,800		
18. Corrected profit in N.A. currency (at.... 1.79.....)	ƒ10,740	ƒ13,962		

19. Indicate under this heading by specifying the division of profit, how the balance of undivided product at the end of the fiscal year connects with the balance of undivided profit at the end of the preceding fiscal year.

20. Further explanation (continue on separate sheet of paper when necessary see headings Nos. 10, 12, 13, 14 and 15)

(a) Comprised of:

Organization Exp.	$ 1,000
Management Fee	" 3,000
Interest on bankloan	" 1,700
Interest on account with broker	" 1,500
Brokers' Commission	" 1,000
Transfer fees	" 1,000
	$ 9,200

N.B. Interest on loan from shareholder and amortization of the cost of acquisition of patent are disallowed as expenses except when specifically allowed in a Tax Ruling by the Inspector of Taxes.

21. Without reservation truthfully answered and signed

...................., ... 19..........

Regarding the obligation to submit copies of the balance sheet and Profit and Loss account or a substitute account reference is made to article 23 of the Profit Tax Ordinance of 1940

Return B

11. Division of Profit

	A Not taxable	B Subject to 1/10 of the rate	C Subject to 15% rate	D Subject to full rate
12. Income				
a. Securities				
1. not taxable (capital gains, etc.)	$(10,000)			
2. taxable			$ 4,000	
b. Interest		$ 6,000		$ 3,000
c. Royalties				
d. Income/compensations art. 14A not being royalties				
e. Taxable income not mentioned under heading 12a through 12d				
f. Total				
g.	$(10,000)	$ 6,000	$ 4,000	$ 3,000
h. Deduction of costs excluding profit tax paid (in case of interest paid indicate entity to which paid in heading no. 20) (Total costs: . . 9,200 (a))	–	" 4,200	" 2,800	" 2,200
Specify computation of allocation of costs under heading no. 20				
i. Profit	$(10,000)	$ 1,800	$ 1,200	$ 800
Article 11(1)				
Article 11(1)				
13. Correction: Profit received share of profit of:				
a. Corporations, societies, companies or foundations as meant in sub paragraph a and b of paragraph 1 of article 1				
b. Entities as meant in sub paragraph .. of paragraph 1 of article 1 which derived at least 9/10 of the entire profit in the N.A. during the year to which the distributed profit applies				
Give specification under heading no. 20				
Article 11(3)				
14. Correction: Profit derived as interest on loans and/or compensation for the use or consumption of goods made available in whatever form to an entity meant in paragraph 1 of article 1 to which capital the body for which the return is filed is entitled.				
Give specification under heading no. 20				
Article 12(1)				

15. Correction: Profit derived from business conducted through a permanent establishment outside the N.A. or from real estate located outside the N.A. and which are subject to tax on profit: a. of business or real estate in The Netherlands or Surinam b. of business or real estate elsewhere Give specification under heading no. 20				
16. Correction				
	$(10, 000)	$ 1, 800	$ 1, 200	$ 800
18. Corrected profit in N.A. currency (at.... 1.79.....)	ƒ(17, 900)	ƒ 3, 222	ƒ 2, 148	ƒ 1, 432

19. Indicate under this heading by specifying the division of profit, how the balance of undivided product at the end of the fiscal year connects with the balance of undivided profit at the end of the preceding fiscal year.

20. Further explanation (continue on separate sheet of paper when necessary see headings Nos. 10, 12, 13, 14 and 15)

(a) Comprised of:

Organization Exp.	$ 1, 000
Management Fee	" 3, 000
Interest on bankloan	" 1, 700
Interest on account with broker	" 1, 500
Brokers' Commission	" 1, 000
Transfer fees	" 1, 000
	$ 9, 200

N. B. Interest on loan from shareholder and amortization of the cost of acquisition of patent are disallowed as expenses except when specifically allowed in a Tax Ruling by the Inspector of Taxes.

21. Without reservation truthfully answered and signed

......................, ... 19..........

Regarding the obligation to submit copies of the balance sheet and Profit and Loss account or a substitute account reference is made to article 23 of the Profit Tax Ordinance of 1940

Finally, assuming the same facts that the dividends and royalties are derived from the United States and the company avails of the Treaty benefits but any of the following conditions are present:

a. the payer of such income is a United States corporation (other than a United States corporation, 60 percent or more of the gross income of which is derived from interest except to the extent derived by a corporation the principal business of which is the making of loans, dividends, royalties, rents from real property, or gain from the sale or other disposition of stock, securities, or real property), 25 percent or more of the stock of which is owned by such entity; or
b. all of the stock of such entity is owned
   (i) solely by one or more individual residents of the Netherlands Antilles in their individual capacities,
   (ii) solely by one or more individual residents of the Netherlands in their individual capacities, or
   (iii) solely by one or more corporations of the Netherlands.[42]

Then, the computation of the Tax will be exactly the same as shown in 'Return A'.

Article 14A: Off-Shore Royalty Income

1. With regard to the income of corporations, as referred to in Article 1, Paragraph 1, under letter a, the objective of which is exclusively or almost exclusively, to derive:

a. income from the alienation or licensing of copyrights, patents, designs, secret processes or formulae, trademarks and analogous property;
b. royalties, including rentals, in respect of motion pictures or in respect of the use of industrial, commercial and scientific equipment, as well as with regard to the exploitation of mines, quarries and other natural resources and real estate;
c. considerations for the rendering of technical assistance;

the profit consisting of the items as referred to hereabove and as far as derived from without the Netherlands Antilles (however, excluding gains made as a result of a change in value or by alienation of property), shall be taxed at one tenth of the rate of Article 15.

2. To arrive at the profit for a fiscal year, the net benefit, derived from the change in value or the alienation of assets as referred to in the foregoing paragraph, shall not be taken into account.

42. Protocol of 1963 revising the U.S.-Netherlands Tax Convention on Double Taxation as extended to the Netherlands Antilles (hereinafter cited as Protocol 1963).

3. At the request of a corporation, the objective of which includes that referred to in Paragraph 1, the Inspector of Taxes may rule that the profits as referred to in Paragraph 1 will be taxed in accordance with the Paragraphs 1 and 2 of this Article, on the conditions to be stipulated by him, at his discretion.

This article was added to the law through the enactment of a law in 1957 referred to as PB 1957-135. In much the same way as the preceding article, the lower taxation privilege granted by the present article may only be availed of by corporations ('NV's').

Patent holding companies deriving income from without the Netherlands Antilles from the sale or licensing of copyrights, patents or secret formulas, and royalties derived by companies for the use of motion pictures, industrial, commercial or scientific equipment as well as real estate rentals are taxed at one/tenth the rates provided for under Article 15, as modified by the Guarantee Law of 1969.

While in general this article refers to passive income, rental of motion pictures (which in other jurisdictions are generally classified as active income or business profits) is classified herein together with other passive-type of income. However, this article being generally applicable to passive income (unless specifically excepted as hereinabove explained) does not cover therefore business profits derived as a result of the operation of hotels or hospitals.

Paragraph 1 under letter a refers to income derived from intangible properties while letter b refers to tangible property including immovable properties. Letter c refers to income derived from services rendered, related to or in connection with, the properties referred to under letters a and b.

In much the same way under Article 14, capital gain is not taxable and capital loss is not deductible. Thus, in the illustration under Article 14 of Tax Returns A and B, it will have been noted that the amortisation of the cost of the acquisition of the patent was not taken into account in the computation of the net taxable income.

Unlike Article 14, however, Article 14A does not prohibit the deduction of interest even though payable to an entity which is a non-banking institution. It is submitted, however, that despite the silence of this article as to the deductibility of a non-bank interest expense, the general prohibition under Article 6, Paragraph 2 under letter c will prevail and therefore interest payable to a person or entity who controls directly or indirectly more than 50 per cent of the issued capital of the company shall not be an allowable deduction.

This article when referring to income derived from intangible assets under letter a of Paragraph 1 refers to alienation of said assets while under letter b, the law is silent regarding income derived from the alienation of tangible assets. Thus, it can be deduced that a company engaged in the development or acquisition of intangible assets for the purpose of sale will be taxed at the lower rates while a company engaged primarily in the acquisition of royalty-producing tangible assets for the sole purpose of trading or resale will be taxed as a trading company rather than a royalty company.

Article 8A: Treaty Country Income

1. A corporation as referred to in Paragraph 1 of Article 1, under letter a, the objective of which is or includes the obtaining of income like dividends, interest and/or royalties, may request that such classes of income be taxed in accordance with the special provisions contained in Paragraph 5 of this article.
2. The request referred to in the foregoing paragraph shall be addressed to the Inspector of Taxes in writing. The Inspector will grant such a request, provided, however, that the decision of the Inspector will only be effective in respect of the fiscal years, which have yet to commence at the time the request is made, unless the Inspector at his discretion decides otherwise.
3. A corporation which, on the strength of the preceding paragraphs, is subject to the provisions of Paragraph 5 of this article, shall remain subject to those provisions, unless a request in writing is made by the corporation to the Inspector of Taxes, to the effect that those provisions cease to apply to it.

The Inspector will grant such a request, provided, however, that the decision of the Inspector shall only be effective in respect of the fiscal years, which have yet to commence at the time the request is made, unless the Inspector at his discretion decides otherwise.

4. The Inspector of Taxes may attach to his grant of a request as referred to in the second and third paragraphs of this article, the condition that the corporation concerned revalues its assets and liabilities as referred to in Paragraph 5 under letter a, at their real value in its balance sheet as of the close of the fiscal year preceding the fiscal year to which the provisions of Paragraph 5 of this article, as the case may be, apply or cease to apply for the first time.
5. The special provisions referred to in the first paragraph are:

a. The profit of the corporation as referred to in Paragraph 1 shall neither include benefits, derived from the changes in value or the alienation of assets, which in essence, produce divi-

43. Official Gazette, 1963, No. 201 (P.B. 1963, No. 201).

dends, interest or royalties as referred to in Paragraph 1, nor those of non-interest bearing claims, credit-balances or debts, which are maintained in connection with those assets.

b. Without prejudice to the provisions of Article 11 and in deviation of the provisions of the second paragraph of Article 15, the profit received as dividends shall be taxed at the rate of 15 per cent.

c. In computing the taxable profits, the following provisions shall apply:
the provisions of Article 14, paragraph 7 under letter a;
the provisions of Article 14, paragraph 8;
the provisions of Article 14, paragraph 11.

Upon the insistence of the United States Government this article was inserted to the Corporate Income Tax Law of 1940 through the enactment of a law in 1963.

Prior to the revision of the Treaty by Protocol in 1963, it will be recalled, dividends, interest, and royalty derived by Netherlands Antilles off-shore companies from the United States were taxed in the Netherlands Antilles at the low rate of 2.4% – 3% pursuant to the provisions of Articles 14 and 14A of the present law.

The US due to the low taxation rates in the Netherlands Antilles has taken the position 'that exemptions and reductions in source taxation provided for by tax treaty are intended only as reciprocal revenue adjustments between governments'.[44] And therefore 'objected to the fact that the benefit of the intergovernmental revenue concession under the treaty in the form of decreases in its statutory tax rate is almost entirely passed on to the Antillean investment companies'.[45] Consequently, in June of 1962 negotiations were conducted in Washington DC between the United States and Antillean delegations to find a solution to the 'Objections that had been raised on the part of the Americans as to the continued granting ... of the special provisions of Articles 13, 14 and 14A'[46] of the present law.

Final negotiations were held in Washington DC between the two governments wherein the Memorandum of Understanding of the two

44. Memorandum of Understanding concerning negotiations for Revision of the Income Tax Convention Between The United States and the Netherlands as applies to The Netherlands Antilles, September 20, 1963, Washington D.C. (hereinafter cited as 'Memorandum of Understanding').
45. See note 44.
46. Explanatory Notes (Memorie van Toelichting) on the Bill to amend the Profit Tax Law of 1940 (P.B. 1955, No. 140) and the Law on Individual Income Taxation of 1943 (P.B. 1956, No. 9) Staten van de Nederlandse Antillen 1963-1964-34, No. 3 (hereinafter cited as MvT 1963-64-34).

Governments reached a conclusion that 'The Antillian delegation has assured the United States delegation that the Netherlands Antilles have no laws enacted before September 1, 1963, which confer substantially similar tax benefits on dividends, interest or royalties.'. However, the Antillian delegation stated that the Netherlands Antilles Government was considering enactment of a new law which would permit Antillian companies to be taxed on dividends from foreign sources at a corporate tax rate of 15 percent. The Antillian delegation asked the opinion of the United States delegation as to whether the 15 percent tax rate being considered would be regarded as a tax benefit 'substantially similar' to the current Antillian tax rate of 2.4 to 3 percent on foreign source dividends. The United States delegation responded that, subject to a review of the actual legislation being considered by the Netherlands Antilles government, its interpretation of Article 1 of the Protocol was that a 15 percent tax rate on dividends would not be a 'substantially similar tax benefit' in view of the fact that a United States withholding tax rate of 15 percent by treaty and an Antillian corporate tax rate of 15 percent combined would produce an overall tax rate on dividends from United States sources of 27.75 percent which would approximate the present United States statutory tax rate of 30 percent.

'The Antillian delegation also asked the opinion of the United States delegation as to whether an increase to 15 percent in the Antillian tax rate on foreign source interest and royalties would be regarded as a "substantially similar tax benefit" in relation to the current Antillian tax rate of 2.4 to 3 percent. The United States delegation responded that its interpretation of Article 1, of the Protocol was that such a tax rate on interest and royalties would be "substantially similar" if this income were not subject to United States tax by treaty since the overall tax rate would only be 15 percent as compared with the present United States statutory tax rate of 30 percent. The Antillian delegation then stated that it assumed that there would be no question of the adequacy of the Antillian tax rate on interest and royalties if such income were taxed no differently than other income of an Antillian corporation is taxed under existing law, which taxes the first 1,000,000 of NA guilders at a 24 percent rate and the remaining income at a 30 percent rate. The United States delegation responded that taxation of interest or royalty income in this manner would not be objectionable in its opinion.'[47] It was on the basis of these negotiations that Article 8A was introduced as part of the Corporate Income Tax Law of the Netherlands Antilles.

The Protocol of 1963 effectively disqualified Netherlands Antilles companies from the benefits of the United States-Netherlands Antilles Treaty if said companies are to avail of the special lower taxation

47. Memorandum of Understanding.

privilege provided for under Articles 13, 14 and 14A of the present law.

The Protocol provided, among others, that

'(1) Articles VII, VIII, and IX of the Convention shall not apply to income derived from sources within the United States by any investment or holding company, corporation, limited partnership or other entity entitled to any of the special tax benefits provided under Article 13, Article 14, or Article 14A of the Netherlands Antilles' National Ordinance on Profit Tax of 1940, as in effect on September 1, 1963, or to substantially similar tax benefits granted under any law of the Netherlands Antilles enacted after such date.' [48]

The enactment of Article 8A gave the Antillean Companies the option to elect taxation under this Article, and continue to benefit from lower taxation at source on dividend (15%) and no withholding tax at a source on Interest and Royalty.

While this Article imposes taxation of United States source dividend at 15% (15% on the net dividend of 85% or an effective rate of 27.75%) and 24-30% rate on United States source Interest and Royalty, the real importance of the present article is contained under Paragraph 5, letter a, which exempts from taxation capital gains and losses.

The first four paragraphs of this Article provide for the procedure on how a company may elect taxation under this article and the conditions laid down for such an election as well as the discretion given by the law to the Inspector of Taxes when granting a request of a company for an election.

Paragraph 5 under letter b provides for the rate of taxation of dividends. The rate of taxation for Interest and Royalty is not provided for under this article as the same is already provided for under Article 15.

Paragraph 5 letter c provides, by reference, the total applicability of the provisions of Article 14 in the computation of the tax.

With reference to the treatment of stock dividends, specific mention is made as to the applicability of Paragraph 11 of Article 14, 'in order to prevent that companies which are subject to Article 14 or 8A, may (in cases where companies have a majority interest in a foreign company, and consequently be in a position to exercise a decisive influence on the manner and substance of its profit distribution) simply appropriate the profits of that foreign company without paying taxes on these profits to the Netherlands Antilles e.g. by means of a distribution of these profits in the form of a stock dividend, followed by a repayment at a later date by the company distributing the stock dividend'. [49]

When the Treaty between the Netherlands and the United Kingdom and Northern Ireland was extended to the Netherlands Antilles by an Exchange of Notes between the two Governments dated the 24th of July, 1970, the application of Articles 13, 14 and 14A of the present

48. Article 1, Protocol of 1963.
49. MvT 1963-64-34.

law was excluded in a similar manner as in the Protocol of the US-NA Treaty described above.

The overall effect of the exclusion of the three articles makes the operation of the Netherlands-UK Treaty similar to the US-NA Treaty with reference to interest and royalty. However, NA corporations, 100% owned by a Netherlands corporation or individuals, or 100% owned by NA residents etc. do not have the effect of lowering taxation in the Netherlands Antilles as is under the US-NA Treaty. With reference to dividends, the adoption of the imputation system in the UK effectively negated whatever benefits the Treaty provides for with reference to taxation at source in the UK for dividends received by NA corporations. The extention of the UK Treaty to the NA took effect on the 1st of January, 1970.

It should be noted that the NA has existing treaty arrangements not only with the US and the UK but also with Denmark and Norway and a special taxation arrangement with The Netherlands.

The treaties with Denmark and Norway and the special taxation arrangement with The Netherlands, unlike the treaties with the US and the UK, do not exclude the low taxation benefits provided for by Articles 14 and 14A of the present law. Thus, dividend income from these three countries is taxed at source at the reduced rate of 15% and the net dividend received in the Netherlands Antilles is taxed at the low rate.

When the interest of the NA company consists of 25% or more of the outstanding shares of the payor of the dividend, the taxation at source is reduced to zero.

National laws of Denmark, Norway and The Netherlands exempt from withholding tax, interest and royalties.

To summarize the taxation of off-shore companies in the Netherlands Antilles, the following flow charts were prepared for purposes of simplification. These charts do not cover income derived by an NA off-shore company from treaty jurisdictions as such income is not governed by the present law. However, income from the Netherlands is covered as the present law deals with Dutch source income.

The definition of passive and active incomes used earlier in this book is applicable for the use of the following flow charts.

The rate of 4.8%-6% given as the taxation rate for income derived by an off-shore company with an active income from abroad (other than The Netherlands or any Treaty country or a jurisdiction wherein the said income has not been subjected to taxation) is a rate granted by Ruling by the Inspector of Taxes.

Interest income derived from The Netherlands secured by realty situated in The Netherlands is taxed in the Netherlands Antilles at 2.4%-3% but by virtue of the tax credit on tax paid in The Netherlands, the effective rate of tax in the NA is zero.

TAXATION RATES OF OFF-SHORE COMPANIES IN THE NETHERLANDS ANTILLES

Chart 3

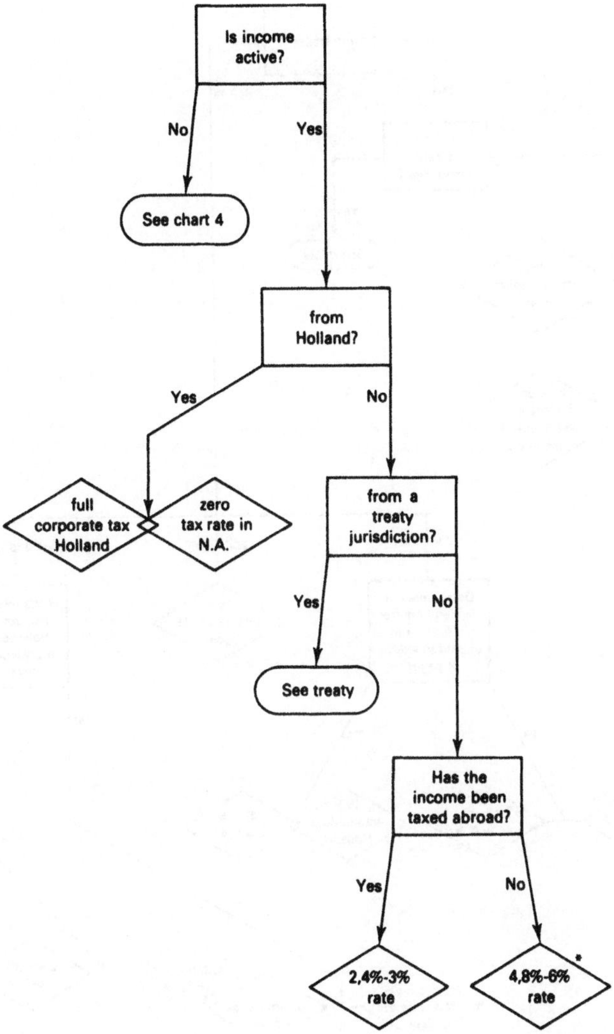

* By virtue of a Tax Ruling

Taxation Rates of Off-shore Companies in the Netherlands Antilles of Passive Income from without the Netherlands Antilles

Chart 4

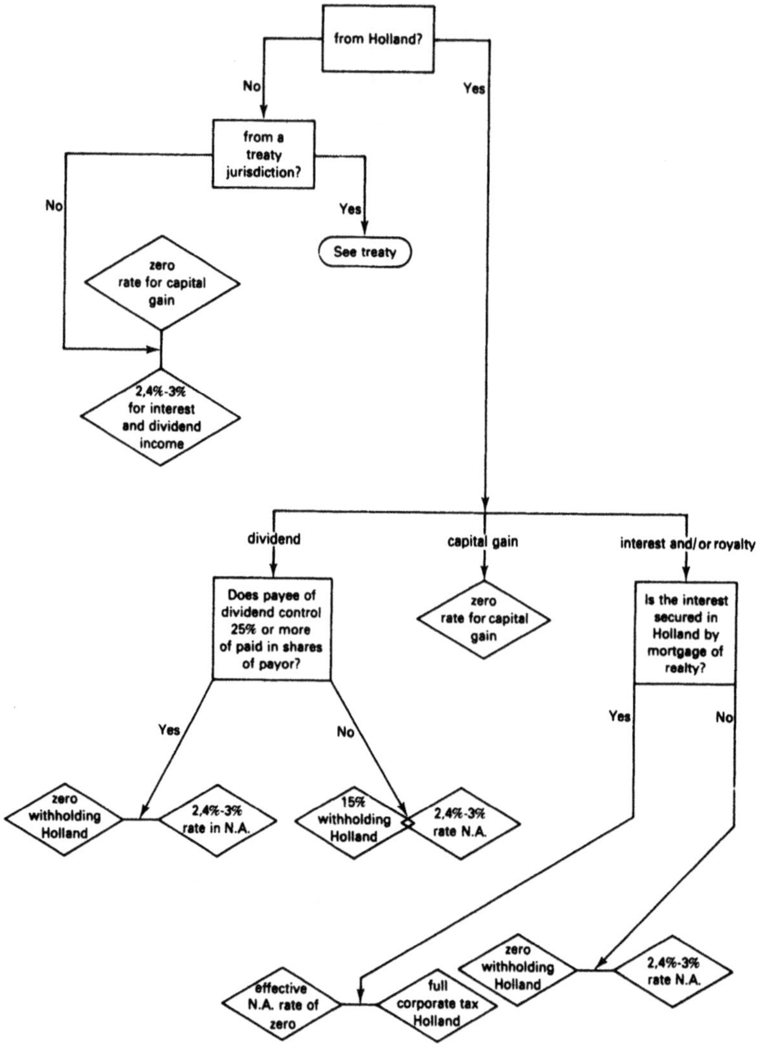

Article 15: Taxation Rates

1. For the application of the tax rates the net taxable income shall be rounded off downwards to the nearest hundred of guilders.
2. The rate of taxation shall be*

Net Taxable Income (NAf)		*Rates of Taxation*	
From	But not exceeding	Minimum tax due	Plus extra percentage for every additional NAf 100
Nil	40,000	–	27
40,000	50,000	10,000	30
50,000	60,000	13,000	33
60,000	70,000	17,100	36
70,000	80,000	20,700	39
80,000	90,000	24,000	41
90,000	100,000	28,700	43
100,000	1,000,000	33,000	33
1,000,000	–	330,000	34

3. For the application of the taxation rates provided under Paragraph 2, the taxable income shall be considered to be constituted as follows:
– the profits which are taxable at the standard rates at the bottom, thereupon the profits which are taxable at one/tenth of the standard rates and finally the profits which are tax exempt, on the top.
4. With regard to corporations as referred to in the Articles 14 and 14A, the taxation rates of Paragraph 2, shall be applied independently to:
– the profits consisting of net income as referred to under Article 14 Paragraph 6 and Article 14A Paragraph 1, and
– the other types of taxable income of such corporations, respectively.

* The schedularized table hereinabove does not appear in the law but is derived from the original enumeration of the law.

Article 16: Liability

1. The tax shall be payable by the taxable corporation, association, company, foundation or entity.
2. The managing directors and managing partners, as well as the representatives within the Netherlands Antilles, shall be jointly and severally liable.

In the event of dissolution or liquidation the persons in charge of the liquidation and their representatives within the Netherlands Antilles shall also be jointly and severally liable. Any of the persons referred to in this paragraph, who upon the demand to pay is able to present to the Inspector satisfactory evidence that he in his capacity is not in a position to handle the payment, shall be relieved of his liability.
3. The evidence must be submitted to the Inspector in writing.
4. Should the Inspector reject the evidence submitted as unsatisfactory, he must state his reasons.
5. A copy of the decision shall be sent to the interested party by registered mail.
6. An appeal against the decision may be lodged with the Court of Tax Appeals within two months after the decision has been mailed.
7. The collection of the tax shall be suspended with regard to anyone on whose behalf evidence is presented as referred to under Paragraph 3:

a. as from the filing until the Inspector's decision or in the event of a rejection by the Inspector of the evidence presented up to the end of the period of two months as referred to under Paragraph 6, unless the interested party will have informed the Inspector in writing, within the last mentioned period, that he does not intend to lodge an appeal of the decision; or
b. until the decision of the Court of Tax Appeals if an appeal has been lodged.

However, it is understood that the Inspector may, at his discretion lift the suspension and authorise the collection of the tax in so far as and in the manner which he deems necessary, if in his opinion the interested party is taking advantage of the period of suspension to take such actions which endanger the possibility of collecting the tax.

8. The terms 'managing directors', 'managing partners', 'administrators in liquidation' and 'representatives' shall include all the persons who at the time the tax liability originated or thereafter have been managing directors, managing partners, administrators in liquidation or representative, even if they would have resigned,

have rendered their account of administration or have been discharged, in the interim, from their liabilities.

This article pinpoints who are principally liable for the payment of the tax and who are jointly and severally liable to such payment. It also provides an exempting circumstance for those who have joint and several liability.

The principal officers of the company i.e. managing directors or partners etc. etc. within the Netherlands Antilles, may be relieved of their joint and several liability if they submit evidence in writing to the Inspector of Taxes to prove that in their capacity they have done all which may be reasonably required of them, but despite such an effort there is a practical impossibility of compliance.

The explanatory note to the draft of the bill on Article 16, defines those persons who should be in a position and therefore be liable for payment of the tax. They are the entity's officers who at the time the tax became due, were the officers who were responsible for the entity's financial affairs and/or the payment of its taxes. While this definition appears to limit the joint and several liability to financial or treasury officers, Article 41 of the present law negates this apparent limitation and in fact expands the coverage of the joint and several liability. Not only are the financial officers liable, but anyone who is employed by the entity within the Netherlands Antilles or any person who may be assumed by the Inspector of Taxes to be in a position, because of his relationship with the taxable entity, to handle the payment of the tax is held to be jointly and severally liable for the payment of the tax.

It should be noted that this joint and several liability for the payment of the tax has, on more than one occasion, been exercised and imposed on local managing directors and liquidators of off-shore companies within the Netherlands Antilles by the Inspector of Taxes.

While this article limits joint and several liability to persons within the Netherlands Antilles, it should further be noted that present treaty arrangements of the Netherlands Antilles with other countries may extend the collection of the tax against officers who are residents of the other treaty jurisdiction, obviously subject to the laws of the other treaty jurisdiction concerning the collection of foreign taxes in such jurisdiction.

Chapters II to IX containing Articles 17 to 55 are procedural provisions of the law which will be treated hereafter simply to acquaint the English reader with their content. The few comments are simply to emphasize certain saliant points as most, if not all, of the Articles are self-explanatory.

Chapter II: Accounting and Tax Return

Article 17: Financial Statements

1. The financial statements and records on the operations of corporations, associations and companies as referred to in Article 1, Paragraph 1 under letter a must be kept in such a manner as will facilitate the determination of the profits derived from the application of the capital employed in and outside the ordinary course of trade or business of such entities.
2. The financial statements and records on the trade or business operations of associations, foundations and other entities as referred to in Article 1 Paragraph 1 under letter b and letter c must be kept in such a manner as will facilitate the determination of the profits derived from such trade or business with reference to entities referred to in Article 1, Paragraph 1, under letter c, the requirement only refers to the trade or business conducted within the Netherlands Antilles.
2. The financial statements and records must be kept in Dutch, English, German, French, Spanish or Papiamentu, while Roman characters and the ordinary corresponding figures must be used.
4. The Inspector may, at his discretion, allow either generally or for individual cases the use of other languages and that the financial statements and records be kept in other characters.
5. The financial statements and records must contain an uninterrupted and current record of the cash situation, registers of debtors, creditors and stocks which are closed each year, as well as annual statements of assets and liabilities.
6. The financial statements and records and their supporting documentation must be preserved for a period of ten years.

The accommodation granted under Paragraphs 3 and 4 to draw up an entity's financial statements in English, German, French or Spanish is a recognition of the limited úse of the Dutch or Papiamentu languages in international commerce.

This article makes it easier for transnational companies with subsidiaries in the Netherlands Antilles to prepare their financial statements.

Article 18: Tax Audit

1. The management of a corporation, and the committee of an association or foundation, or other entity, whenever so requested, are under the obligation to allow the Inspector, or one or more officials designated by the Inspector to conduct the investigation, or one or more experts or interpreters appointed pursuant to Article 42, to examine the books financial statements and records, and their supporting documentation.
2. The Inspector may at his discretion issue additional regulations on the investigation of the books and records and their supporting documentation and concerning the place where such investigation shall be conducted.

Article 19: Issuance of Tax Returns

1. In order that an assessment may be made, the management of a corporation, and the committee of an association or foundation, or other entity shall be requested to file a tax return; such a request shall be made by sending to the taxable entity the necessary tax return form in duplicate, by registered mail.
2. The management or committee may notify the Inspector on its own accord that it wishes to file a tax return in which case the necessary form shall be issued to it, in duplicate.
3. Except in the case of a request of the management or committee, the inspector shall not issue tax return forms:

a. prior to the expiration of a period of two months after the close of the fiscal taxable year, in so far as an entity as referred to in Article 8 or 9 is concerned;
b. prior to the expiration of a period of four months after the close of the entity's fiscal taxable year, in so far as other entities are concerned.

The amendment of Article 9 making the oil processing industry in the Netherlands Antilles taxable like any other corporation except for the provision on minimum tax, did not carry a corresponding amendment of Paragraph 3 letter a of this article. Consequently, Paragraph 3 under letter a, is no longer applicable insofar as it refers to Article 9.

Article 20: Tax Return

1. The tax return shall consist of a statement containing:
a. appropriate information showing whether or not the entity has made profits and if so, the amount of such profits;
b. any additional particulars which will be or may be necessary or useful for the implementation of the present law.
2. The models for the tax return forms shall be determined by National Decree.
3. The distribution of the tax return forms is entrusted to the Inspector.
4. Each tax return form shall bear the date on which such form was issued.

Article 21: Signing of the Tax Return

1. The management or committee of the corporation, association, company, foundation or other entity to which a tax return form has been issued in duplicate, is under the obligation to fill out one of the forms, explicitly, unequivocally and without withholding the truth, and – if necessary after having dealt with the duplicate copy in the manner pursuant to Article 24 – to sign the same.
2. The tax return may be filed on behalf of the management or committee by a person authorized thereto in writing, provided that the tax return is submitted accompanied by such authorization.

Article 22: Period for Filing

1. One of the tax return forms, must be returned to the Inspector of Taxes within sixty days after its date of issue.
2. Upon request a receipt shall be issued free of charge.
3. The Inspector may, at his discretion, allow an extension of the period for filing.
4. In the event of loss, new tax return forms shall be issued free of charge.

An extention of time to file a return is also implicitly provided for under Article 24 at the discretion of the Inspector. After the lapse of the extention period, the provisions of Article 24 are made to apply.

Article 23: Enclosures

1. The tax return must be accompanied by the following:
a. a copy of the balance sheet and the profit and loss account pertaining to the fiscal year, together with a copy of the report rendered to – as the case may be – the shareholders, members and other interested parties, of the corporation, association, company, foundation or entity;
b. insofar as the business as referred to under Article 17, Paragraph 2 is concerned – a copy of the balance sheet, and profit and loss account pertaining to such year;
c. a copy of the deed of incorporation and of any deeds of amendment thereof, unless such documents have already been submitted with a previous tax return.
2. If, instead of a balance sheet and profit and loss account, an account in another form has been prepared, a copy of such account must be submitted together with the tax return.
3. The copies must – as the case may be – be authenticated by the management or committee of the corporation, association, foundation or other entity, by means of a signed or certified statement on these copies.
4. The Inspector may, at his discretion, accept certified extracts.

Corporations which are taxable only in another jurisdiction by virtue of treaty arrangement, e.g. realty companies doing trade or business in the US through a permanent establishment, are sometimes permitted under Paragraph 2 of this article to file together with their return in the Netherlands Antilles a copy of their tax return as filed in the US with the statement that the corporation is taxable only in the US. However, this is discretionary on the part of the Inspector. If there is any income other than realty income a balance sheet and a profit and loss account is often required in the Netherlands Antilles.

Article 24: Provisional Return

1. If after the expiration of the period mentioned under Article 22, or as the case may be, any extension thereof, the information referred to under Article 20 Paragraph 1, under letter a should not have become available to the management of the corporation, association, company, foundation or entity it must estimate the profits to the best of its knowledge and file a provisional return accordingly.

2. The provisions of Articles 20 Paragraph 1, Articles 21 and 22 Paragraph 2 shall apply correspondingly.
3. A tax return must then be filed within two months after the financial statements will have been determined, however, not later than by the end of the next year.
4. The Inspector may extend the period referred to in the preceding paragraph.

A provisional return filed pursuant to this Article, in practice, is identical with the return filed for the previous fiscal year rather than an estimate of the tax for the present taxable fiscal year.

Chapter III: Tax Assessments

Article 25: Tax Assessments; Supplementary Information

1. Tax assessments are made by the Inspector.
2. Without prejudice to its obligation to allow the investigation of the financial statements and records, and their supporting documentation pursuant to the provisions of Article 18, the management of the corporation, association, company, foundation or entity may be invited by or on behalf of the Inspector to submit supplementary information either verbally or in writing and to allow the investigation of further documents and other papers, all for the purpose of the verification of the tax return or any supplementary representations made.

Article 26: Failure to File – Penalty

1. Should a tax return not be filed notwithstanding the issuance of the tax return form and notwithstanding summons in writing or in case of failure to comply with the obligations to allow the investigation of the financial statements and records, and their supporting documentation for the purpose of the assessment, then the amount of the tax may be increased by not more than one hundred percent.
2. Unless satisfactory evidence to the contrary is submitted, the issuance of the tax return form in the name of a corporation, association, company, foundation or entity shall be deemed to have been received by the management and the financial statements and records and their supporting documentation shall be considered to be in the possession of such management.

Article 27: Assessment before Fiscal Year-End

1. The Inspector may make an assessment before the close of a fiscal year in such an amount he may deem reasonable:

a. in the event of dissolution, termination, liquidation or bankruptcy;
b. in the event of the discontinuance or a considerable reduction of the business activities, or in the event of the alienation of real property situated within the Netherlands Antilles or rights attached to such property;
c. with respect to the profits of entities which are not based in the Netherlands Antilles and which are only temporarily carrying on a trade or business within the Netherlands Antilles.

2. The provisional assessment shall be considered as an assessment referred to in this law solely for the purpose of the collection of the tax and for the purpose of the provisions of Chapter IV.
3. The Inspector shall have the authority to reduce or make a supplementary provisional assessment at his discretion, whenever the assessment should prove incorrect.

Article 28: Provisional Assessment

1. When a provisional return is filed pending final assessment, a provisional assessment may be made.
2. Should the tax provisionally assessed on the basis of the return filed, be more than 25 percent less than the tax which would be due according to the mandatory tax return, then the amount of the tax shall be assessed at an amount determined on the basis of the final return increased by an interest of one half of one percent per month of the difference, over the period starting on the day on which provisional return has been filed and ending on the day in which the final return was filed; for the purposes of this paragraph the period shall be rounded off upward to a full month or full months.
3. Nothwithstanding the provisions of Article 24 if no provisional return has been filed, a provisional assessment may be made, in an amount corresponding with the tax computed on the basis of the final return filed, increased by the interest calculated in the manner as described under Paragraph 2.
4. In case no tax return is filed, the computation of the interest shall be based on the amount assessed in accordance with Article 26 on the date an assessment is made.
5. Should the assessment referred to in the preceding paragraph be revised by operation of Article 31 or 44, or reduced by a decision of the Court of Tax Appeals, then the interest shall be readjusted.
6. A provisional assessment shall be considered as final assess-

ment within the meaning of this law solely for the purpose of the collection of the tax.

Article 29: Settlement of Final Assessment with Provisional Assessment

1. If the amount of the provisional assessment made pursuant to Articles 27 or 28 be equal to the amount of the final assessment, then the later shall not be collected. If the amount of the final assessment be less than the provisional assessment, then no tax shall be collected on such final assessment and the amount of the provisional assessment shall be reduced correspondingly.
2. Should the amount of the final assessment be equal to or be lower than the amount of the provisional assessment, then the management or committee of the corporation, association, company, foundation or entity shall be notified accordingly in writing under date.

Chapter IV: Objections to Tax Assessments

Article 30: Objections

1. Objections to an assessment may be made within two months from the date of the assessment. For entities situated abroad the time limit shall be four months.
2. The management or committee of the corporation, association, company, foundation or entity must file a letter of objections with the Inspector.
3. Persons authorized in writing may file the letter of objection for and on behalf of the management or committee, provided, the written authority is submitted with the objections.
4. If so requested a receipt shall be issued for the letter of objections filed, free of charge.

There is no formal form to file the objections to the assessment. A letter stating the objections to the assessment made, filed within two months by Netherlands Antilles entities and four months by entities based without the Netherlands Antilles, shall be sufficient.

Article 31: Decision on the Objections

1. The letter of objections shall be decided upon by the Inspector.
2. In case the Inspector finds the objections justified, he shall reassess the taxable amount, thereby taking into consideration any and all errors in the tax assessment he acknowledges.
3. In the event that the objections are rejected totally or partially the decision shall state the grounds for the decision.
4. A copy of the decision shall be sent to the plaintiff by registered mail.

Article 32: Appeal

A plaintiff who is not satisfied with the decision rendered on his letter of objections may lodge an appeal with the Court of Tax Appeals within two months from the date the copy of the decision was mailed. For assessed entities situated abroad the period shall be four months.

The Court of Tax Appeals is not a court of original but of appellate jurisdiction. Petitions for injunctions or declaratory relief against the collector on tax cases are filed with the ordinary courts.

Chapter V: Supplemental Assessments

Article 33: Supplemental Assessment

1. In case of additional information subsequently available, it is established that a lower amount of tax has been assessed, a supplemental assessment may be made provided five years have not elapsed from the close of the fiscal year under review.
2. Under similar conditions, a supplemental assessment may be made in case the final assessment has been incorrectly reduced or voided or in case the Inspector has incorrectly decided to refrain from making an assessment.

Article 34: Clarification of the Additional Information

1. Supplemental assessments are made by the Inspector.
2. Prior to making a supplemental assessment the Inspector shall grant the management or committee of the corporation, association, company, foundation or entity to clarify the additional information which has subsequently become available.

Article 35: Increase

1. The tax payable in the supplemental assessment shall be increased by one hundred percent.
2. There shall be no increase if the supplemental assessment is based on voluntary written information supplied by the management or committee of the corporation, association, company, foundation or entity unless such information was furnished after the management or committee was required to furnish information or to allow the inspection of the books and records.

Article 36: Objections

> Objections to a supplemental assessment may be lodged with the Court of Tax Appeals within two months from the date of the notice of assessment. For assessed entities situated abroad, the period shall be four months.

Notwithstanding the language of Article 35 Paragraph 1 the one hundred percent increase in the supplemental assessment is not mandatory.

Unlike the appeal on a formal assessment wherein an objection must first be filed with the Inspector of Taxes and after such an objection is denied, an appeal may be made to the Court of Tax Appeals, objections to supplemental assessments are made directly to the Court of Tax Appeals without the need of filing a letter of objections to the supplemental assessment with the Inspector of Taxes.

Chapter VI: Collection

Article 37: Administrative Procedure

1. The Inspector shall enter tax assessments on a register.
2. As soon as possible the Inspector shall forward the register to the collectors charged with the collection of the tax. The Collector shall notify the management or committee of the corporation, association, company, foundation or entity by means of a dated notice of assessment by registered mail.
3. The notice of assessment shall be delivered in a sealed envelope.
4. When the notice of assessment is submitted upon payment in a sealed envelope, the same shall be returned in a similar manner after the payment is recorded thereon.

Article 38: Period of Payment

The assessed amount must be paid within two months from the date marked on the notice of assessment.

Article 39: Collectibility in the Event of Dissolution etc.

The amount assessed shall be collectable immediately in the cases referred to under the first paragraph of Article 27.

Chapter VII: Special Provisions

Article 40: The Terms 'Management' and 'Committee'

For the purposes of this law the terms 'management' and 'committee' shall include managing partners, representatives in the Netherlands Antilles, and in case of liquidation or dissolution, any person in charge of the liquidation and their representatives in the Netherlands Antilles.

Article 41: Designation as Representative

1. Any person in this country who is employed by or acts on behalf of and for the benefit of a corporation, association, company, foundation or entity as referred to in Article 1, or in case of dissolution or liquidation – any person in charge of the liquidation may be designated by the Director of Taxes as the representatives of such entity within the context of the preceding Article, after having been given the opportunity to state his objections.
2. Whenever any person or persons other than those mentioned under Article 16 are designated by virtue of their relationship with the corporation, association, company, foundation or entity can be presumed to be in a position to handle the payment of the taxes due, they shall be notified accordingly at the time they are so designated; upon notification to such person, the provisions of this law relating to the liability shall become applicable.

Article 42: Designation of Experts and Interpreters

1. The Inspector may designate experts and interpreters in order to investigate the financial statements and other papers.
2. Prior to the assumption of their duties, the experts and interpreters shall take an oath before the Governor of the Netherlands Antilles to the effect that they will perform their duties honestly, conscientiously and to the best of their knowledge and abilities.

3. The experts and interpreters as referred to under Paragraph 1, may be granted a remuneration in accordance with general regulations determined by National Decree.

Article 43: Secrecy of Information

1. It shall be unlawful for any person who, in the exercise of his duties pursuant to this law, has gained knowledge of any facts or to whom an information has been disclosed in respect of the affairs or activities of whomsoever, to divulge such facts or information any further than is required in the performance of such duties.
2. The prohibition in this Article shall also apply to the experts and interpreters referred to in the preceding Article.

This article provides for the secrecy of the information revealed by the taxpayer to the Inspectorate of Taxes. Article 48 of the present law provides for the penal sanctions in case of violation of the present Article.

Article 44: Revision of Assessments ex Officio

Incorrect assessments may be reduced or annulled by the Inspector, ex officio.

Article 45: Additional Regulations

1. The Minister of Finance is authorized:
   a. to issue additional regulations for the implementation of this law, if and in so far as this law does not provide for otherwise:
   b. to wholly or partially remit a tax assessed, in cases of exceptional errors or excusable omissions.
2. The Inspector shall be charged with the execution of the decisions of the Ministers of Finance.

This Article, by implication, provides for administrative appeal to the Minister of Finance in case of errors and excusable omissions.

Chapter VIII: Penal Provisions

Article 46: Filing an Incorrect or Incomplete Tax Return

1. Any person who intentionally files an incorrect or incomplete tax return as referred to under Chapter II, if any loss for the Netherlands Antilles may result therefrom, shall suffer imprisonment of not more than six months.
2. The provision of Paragraph 1 shall not apply if the person who has filed the return, on his own volition, but before the Public Prosecutor has been notified, files a correct and complete return provided: an assessment has not yet been made and, provided further, the Inspector has neither made objections to the return filed nor invited the management or committee of the corporation, association, company, foundation or entity to provide information or other papers, or, an assessment has been made for too low an amount.

Article 47: Submitting False or Forged Papers

Any person who intentionally submits or produces for investigation by the Inspector or a civil servant designated by the Inspector to investigate the books and records and supporting documentation or an expert or interpreter designated pursuant to Article 42, any false or forged papers as if they were genuine and not forged, shall suffer imprisonment of not more than two years.

Article 48: Violation of the Secrecy

1. Any person who intentionally violates the secrecy mandated by Article 43 shall suffer imprisonment of not more than six months or be fined not more than six hundred guilders.
2. Any person who has caused the violation of the secrecy shall suffer imprisonment of not more than three months or be fined not more than three hundred guilders.

3. No prosecution shall be commenced unless a complaint is filed by the person whose secrecy has been violated.

Article 49: Criminal Offence

All acts punishable under this law shall be considered a criminal offence.

Article 50: Supplemental Assessment after Conviction

1. When a conviction rendered pursuant to Article 46 has become final, a supplemental assessment shall be made even after the expiration of the period provided for under Article 33.
2. To this, Article 34, Paragraph 2, is not applicable.

Article 51: Responsibility for the Investigation

The persons designated under Article 8 numbers 1 to 4 inclusive of the Code of Criminal Procedure and the civil servants charged with the implementation of this law shall be responsible for the investigation of the offences committed against this law.

Chapter IX: Transitory and Final Provisions

Article 52: Transitory Provisions

1. The tax shall be levied for the first time in respect of the year ending June 30, 1939.
2. For the application of Article 10 the years ending prior to July 1, 1939 shall also be taken into consideration.
3. The tax due for the first year ending after June 30, 1939 pursuant to Paragraph 1 shall be reduced by the amount paid in respect of distributions of profits of the same year pursuant to the Income Tax Law of 1906.
4. Notwithstanding the provisions of this article the fiscal year as determined pursuant to Article 27 number 1 of the Income Tax Law of 1940 shall continue to be effective in respect of entities which were not based in Curaçao, Aruba or Bonaire as at May 1, 1940 and which were carrying on a trade or business (other than the insurance business) in one or more of these islands either directly or through authorized representatives and which were subject to the provisions of the Income Tax Law of 1906 with respect to the last year to which the latter law would have been applicable in the year ended April 30, 1940.

Article 53: Repeal of the Income Tax Law 1906 as to the Taxation of Entities

As from May 1, 1940 the provisions of the Income Tax law of 1906 (as amended up to and including the amendment by the law of March 1, 1938 published in the Official Gazette 1938, No. 21) will not apply as to the taxation of corporations, associations, companies, foundations and entities as referred to under Article 1, except for the tax due for the fiscal years which have commenced prior to that date.

Article 54: Exemptions – Stamp Duties

All papers regarding the implementation of this law or resulting from such implementation shall be exempt from stamp duty and shall be registered without charge should such papers be subject of compulsory registration.

Article 55: Taking Effect; Title

1. This law shall take effect on May 1, 1940.
2. The law may be referred to as: 'Landsverordening op de Winstbelasting 1940'.

Index

INDEX

INDEX

INDEX

GPSR Compliance

The European Union's (EU) General Product Safety Regulation (GPSR) is a set of rules that requires consumer products to be safe and our obligations to ensure this.

If you have any concerns about our products, you can contact us on ProductSafety@springernature.com

In case Publisher is established outside the EU, the EU authorized representative is:

Springer Nature Customer Service Center GmbH
Europaplatz 3
69115 Heidelberg, Germany

Batch number: 10844827

Printed by Printforce, the Netherlands